housebeautiful

Outdoor Living and Gardens

housebeautiful

OUTDOOR LIVING AND GARDENS

TEXT BY

ELVIN MCDONALD

HEARST BOOKS
NEW YORK

Library of Congress Catalog Card Number: 89-81525
ISBN: 1-58816-042-4 (paperback)
        0-688-09429-5 (hardcover)

Front cover photograph by Elyse Lewin
Back cover photographs (clockwise from top left) by Elyse Lewin,
William P. Steele, Joshua Green, Lilo Raymond

Produced by Smallwood & Stewart, Inc., New York City
Interior design: MARY FORSELL
Cover design: DEBORAH KERNER

Printed in China
First Paperback Edition 2001

1 2 3 4 5 6 7 8 9 10

www.housebeautiful.com

CONTENTS

INTRODUCTION
10

CHAPTER ONE

Outdoor Rooms
13

CHAPTER TWO

Entrances
41

CHAPTER THREE

Porches & Patios
69

CHAPTER FOUR

Swimming Pools
115

CHAPTER FIVE

Little Retreats
139

CHAPTER SIX

Gardens
167

RESOURCE DIRECTORY
210

PHOTOGRAPHY CREDITS
222

INTRODUCTION

As much as I love houses, my favorite spaces have always been outdoors. The first bright morning in March I'll dust the snow off the terrace and coerce my reluctant family into an out-of-season picnic. When housebound on January's dreary days, I'll savor the outdoors vicariously by leafing through a pile of seed and flower catalogs. And on a hot July afternoon, what could be more blissful than sipping cool lemonade on a wide, shady porch?

There's a magic to the outdoors that the inside of a house—bounded by walls and doors—can never have. A flower bed lifts the spirits; a hidden corner becomes a secret garden; a tea party in a pergola evokes the charm of the Victorian age. That's the purpose of this book—to encourage you to think of *your* outdoor spaces not just as backyard and front yard but as extensions of your home, and to recognize all the delights and endless possibilities that lie right outside. There's no reason why porches, balconies and arbors shouldn't have all the comforts of home—and more. Whether your fancy runs toward a tiny container garden in the city or a meadow abloom with wild flowers, this book can help you endow your outdoor spaces with the best of interior and landscape design.

The term "landscape" may seem intimidating to some, but it needn't be, as these pages prove. Depending on what you want—a showplace garden or a quiet corner for relaxation and reflection—making the most of the outdoors can be as easy as plopping an inviting Adirondack chair beneath a shady tree. The secret is to approach the outside of your home as you would the inside, seeing it as a series of separate "rooms" that you design and decorate.

What you do with your outdoor spaces can add enrichment to your home. The charming corner garden you'll find in Chapter Six, for example, was once a little-used back entryway. Now it's the homeowner's favorite retreat. The look of your front entrance sets the tone for your entire house, providing a note of welcome for anyone who comes to see you. In back, your deck or patio can be made to seem either a cozy or expansive addition to the shell of your house, and if you're lucky enough to have a pool, you may never want to leave home.

I must confess that my favorite outdoor "rooms" are porches (screened, open or enclosed) and terraces. To me they offer the best of both outdoors and in. That's one reason they are such fun to decorate and so pleasant to spend time in. Looking at the sun-washed porch in Chapter Three, I can see myself spending hour after hour curled up with a book, enjoying soft breezes.

As you'll find as you experience this book, few people have outdoor spaces that are entirely problem-free. If anything, problems can be seen as challenges forcing us to make our spaces even more imaginative and special. Nancy McCabe solved the problem of a steeply sloping yard by turning it into a charming two-tiered garden. And lacking space for a large garden outdoors, Londoner Ken Turner created a garden inside his city home with a floral tablecloth and slipcover and a bounty of potted blooms.

Outdoor decorating's greatest virtue is in offering endless room for creativity. What could be more en-chanting than an old well-sweep pointing the way to a profusion of lilies just beyond it? Or more whimsical than Mary Emmerling's folk art flag gate?

Outdoor decorating touches may be as simple or as elaborate as you wish. A window box of bright sun-flowers says summer as successfully as designer John Saladino's wonderful boathouse patio and its terrycloth-covered chairs.

But as much as this book is meant to enlighten and inspire, it also offers a wonderful escape. Though few of us may have an old, windowless greenhouse like the one in Chapter One, wrapped in an awning of creeping roses, we can capture the same romantic air by building a small arbor and planting our own roses. Anything is possible if we just stretch our imagination.

So pull up a chair and get ready to dream.

THE EDITORS OF *House Beautiful*

CHAPTER ONE

OUTDOOR ROOMS

People are accustomed to thinking of decorating in terms of interior spaces. So when they approach the garden as a room that is located outdoors, it becomes easier to design its components. Ground covers and paths are analogous to floors and halls; hedges, fences and other vertical boundaries serve as walls; and tree canopies and the sky itself comprise the ceiling.

The furniture of the outdoor room is similar to the interior type, although it tends to be portable and weatherproof. Accessories such as fountains, statuary and container plantings are also similar to their indoor counterparts—items meant to add visual interest while also evoking the design sensibility of the garden's owner. The plants themselves define areas of the yard and add color and texture to the landscape.

As you set about to design a garden as a room outdoors, remember that it takes time to absorb all of the possibilities. Before going ahead with full-scale landscaping, take time to sketch out a design. Then, as your vision of the outdoor room and how its components interrelate takes shape, create a more detailed plan. Some people feel comfortable making the design decisions for the yard themselves; others prefer to consult a landscape architect. But even without the help of an expert, it's possible to completely transform an outdoor space simply by working with what's there and finding ways to use the natural terrain to best advantage.

Simplicity may serve you better than anything complicated. The light touch should always be cultivated, for none of this need be a chore. American landscape architect Ellen Shipman set out this simple recipe for a garden in 1929: "A wall, a path, a coping around the bed, a tree, a place to sit—that is a garden." The design and arrangement of these elements should express a personal style that is harmonious with that of the house.

◆ Perched on its own small patio (*previous page*) surrounded by lush evergreens, flowers and grasses, an Adirondack chair sits in solitary splendor near a protected latticework arbor. This is a place to think grand thoughts, or just ponder the roses, depending on the hour.

◆ The best way to decide where to put a deck is this: Look for worn patches of grass. This shady spot (*opposite*) under the backyard sycamore tree was such a favorite place for eating even before the deck was built that the grass was starting to wear away. So it was only logical to lay some decking here, dance-floor style, to make the picnic area more official—and save the lawn in the process. The old round table with checkered cloth is left out all the time; after a rain, the sun dries the cloth in an instant. On the table, a stoneware crock has a bouquet of cosmos from the gardens beyond. Overhead, a tiny finch holds forth from a brass bird cage. A bench that was once a regular in the dining room (*above*) is now host to outdoor meals.

The first step in designing for the outdoors is thinking of the yard as not just one outdoor room, but several. Each can have its own function and style, but they should be harmonious in design so they seamlessly blend together in the landscape. A practical approach to making sure your yard's design meets your needs is to make a list of all the functions that it should serve and plan accordingly.

You probably want to designate an area for dining and entertaining, and this usually is the patio or back porch. Decorate this room with the same types of pretty ornaments that catch the eye in the dining room—vases of brightly colored flowers, sprightly tablecloths and attractive yet durable furniture. Whimsical touches like birdhouses, wind chimes and pretty flower-filled containers welcome guests to the dining area.

Room for a garden is always essential. Vegetable and herb gardens can be decorative as well as utilitarian, and there's no reason to hide such gardens in remote areas of the property. Usually, they are organized in neat geometric patterns so that it is easy to harvest their delicious bounty. Consider creating a wigwam of bamboo or tomato stakes on which pole beans can climb. These can be drawn together at the top and tied, which creates a striking, almost sculptural effect.

Unless a flower garden is meant to be a secret, private space, it should be located where it can be seen and enjoyed. Not only should you consider how the garden fits into its outdoor surroundings, but how it is viewed from within the house. If you have a second-story porch or terrace, you might locate a flower garden below to make the view from above even more pleasant.

It's possible to have a combination of garden styles on a property. Contrasting garden styles tend to heighten each other's effects. A wild, overgrown mélange of plants can be contained within a neatly contoured border. Or a very formal garden can give way to a wooded area. An expanse of grass between the formal garden and the natural garden allows for a smooth transition between the two styles.

When designing any garden, think of the whole as a composition. Just as you would create a balance indoors between solid, structural items and soft furnishings, in the outdoors colors, textures and shapes should harmonize. A border of brightly colored flowers is tempered by the neutralizing effects of a green lawn or shrubbery. Low-growing flowers need to be balanced by more vertical elements, such as trees.

To add visual interest to a garden and offset the soft quality of plants, add small rocks and boulders with unusual shapes and textures. Architectural plants such as evergreens provide horizontal and vertical definition, particularly when they are sheared into neat forms. It is also important to achieve a balance of plants and structures, such as walkways, benches and pergolas.

◆ A high beamed ceiling and generous oversize windows keep artist Beverlye Hyman's studio (*opposite*) on the same scale as the trees that surround it. In a whimsical structure such as this, the weather is as much a part of the design as any tangible element.

◆ This scene of the studio across a landscaped lawn (*above*) is framed by magnificent oaks. Outside, approaching the studio, gnarled old oak trees with their arms akimbo scrabble down a hillside (*right*). The trees line a meandering garden path that weaves through ferns and hostas.

◆ Designing an upper lawn and a lower lawn was garden designer Nancy McCabe's way of coping with a very steep backyard. Dividing the lawn doubled her opportunity to create two different outdoor environments. Most activities—sunbathing, reading, picnicking—center on the house and attached greenhouse (*left*). So that's where the chaise, umbrella and assorted chairs have landed, along with a number of potted plants and scented geranium standards that hug the side of the house. The latticework over the back doorway supports a flourishing sweet autumn clematis, and at its foot an urn (*left, below*) sprouts abundant foliage and richly fragrant heliotrope flowers. Pots of gray-leaved artemesia mark the twin stairways of the lower yard (*opposite*). Here, the mood is more tranquil. A symmetrically designed border garden outlines the perimeter of the property and provides plenty of bouquets to fill the house from springtime through early fall.

◆ In the Napa Valley, not only leaves change color with the seasons, so do the meadow flowers. The double-story veranda of this handsome farmhouse (*opposite, above and below*) offers orchestra seats to this benign spectacle. The meadow out front is filled with one flower show after another, from the blue bonnets and golden mustard of spring to the Indian paintbrush and daisies of summer. Whatever the time of year, though, the yard is virtually maintenance-free.

◆ Generous drifts of daisies mixed with purple loosestrife and yarrow (*above*) are scattered across the field, within sight of the raised front porch of this house. These kinds of flower meadows work best with native varieties that will blend easily into an informal landscape. To preserve its natural appearance, the grass is mown only twice a year, at the very beginning and end of summer.

The traditional emerald-green lawn is a lovely garden element on formal properties, but doesn't always look at home in yards with a more relaxed landscaping style. There is, however, a middle ground between clipped formality and an overgrown jungle of plants. A wilder-looking lawn can be achieved simply by allowing the grass to grow a bit and not weeding out wild flowers and other interesting invaders that naturally take root. This approach is appreciated by gardeners who would rather spend time perfecting the flower border than endlessly weeding a lawn. If your property is sizable, the wild lawn is an especially nice choice, as its open expanse suggests a Midwestern prairie and also looks striking in wintertime.

A more direct approach to a natural-looking yard is to plant a meadow lawn, easily achieved with a combination flower-and-seed mix. Meadow lawns usually include native wildflowers, which thrive naturally in the yard, and so won't demand upkeep in your spare time.

Attractive accompaniments to the untamed lawn are rustic Western-style fences, meandering and overgrown pathways and wooded areas alive with birds and decorated with nature's own ornaments: mossy logs, evergreen needles and pine cones and trees with especially unusual forms and bark textures.

◆ Not the least of the pleasures of the outdoor room is, of course, the flower garden. The textures, forms and above all the palette of nature provide limitless scope for creating moods ranging from the wild abundance of an informal garden to the strict symmetry of an ordered property. Color generally shapes our first, and often our most powerful, impressions. On a Long Island, New York, property (*opposite*), designer J. Crawford contrasts the blues of veronicas and campanulas with ruffled milk-white peonies.

◆ An arched gateway leads to a colorful entrance garden designed by Nat Norris (*above*), which welcomes visitors with its friendly informality. Inside, flowers and vines are encouraged to spill randomly over the brick walls and paths. Poppies, foxgloves, blue and white delphiniums, roses and bearded irises form strong vertical accents, while the wall is home to various plants suited to the rockery.

The most obvious way of creating a room outdoors is to erect actual boundaries between different areas of the property. Any number of devices can be employed to create these divisions. One or more walls of a given outdoor room may be provided by the house or another building. High walls that are solid can effectively trap every degree of warmth in a cold season. By the same token, high walls can be a liability in hot weather unless openings are provided to capture breezes and effect cooling. Low walls can afford extra seating, or act as a sideboard on which to serve food and drink. Enterprising gardeners can use this space for displaying container plantings, stylish topiaries or a collection of bonsai. Always bear in mind that exterior walls tend to create pockets of sun on one side and cooler, shadier situations on the other. This holds true whether they are constructed or made from living hedges.

The courtyard garden is the quintessential outdoor room because it is distinctly defined on all sides by walls. Living walls may entirely enclose the courtyard or be used in combination with constructed portions. Plants may be shrubs, trees or vines, evergreen or deciduous, flowering or nonflowering. Both the design and the kind of plant used help determine whether the wall is trained and maintained formally or informally.

The formal hedge comprising one specific kind of plant is perhaps the most easily planted and maintained, and sculpting these hedges into a multitude of forms is a satisfying activity that is both art and craft. Formal, clipped hedge walls may also combine two or more distinct species, perhaps a plain green holly and one with variegated leaves. Evergreen hedges are classically comprised of yew. Creating a hedge that is a combination of evergreen and a deciduous plant, such as beech, offers contrasting texture and color in all seasons.

◆ Birds and bees are equally at home in a courtyard garden, one of several on the grounds of this estate (*right*). The tile-roofed outbuilding harbors a dovecote in its upper reaches, and birds that find no vacancy there build their nests in the high green hedge. It's been allowed to grow unchecked for years, to give this area a little extra seclusion. Roses fill the air with their soft scent, and the bees that gather nectar here have only a short hop to their hives, located on another part of the property.

Plants best suited to formal, clipped hedge walls are those cultivated primarily for the effect of foliage. Flowering shrubs such as forsythia and azalea, lilac and spirea are robbed of their glory by clipping. They belong in the informal hedge wall, massed in groups of one type of plant or interwoven in a changing tapestry of colors and textures with something always blooming to delight the eye. Honeysuckle, mock orange, hedge rose and jasmine can be interplanted in hedges to bring fragrance into the garden.

Fences are the traditional choice to divide and define areas of property. If the fence must serve practical purposes, such as keeping small children safely within its boundaries or creating a sense of privacy, then it should be solid and high. Wooden fences are good choices for this purpose, as they are both attractive and serviceable. It's possible to vary the pattern of the boards in the fence to create a decorative effect. For example, the lower area of the fence can be composed of vertical boards and the upper section can be made of diagonally oriented slats of wood. If you prefer to erect a metal fence on account of its durability, you can soften its look by training vines or espaliering shrubbery along it. Fences used only to define areas of the yard can be as decorative and open as you wish. The split-rail

◆ A split-rail fence is like a friendly, beckoning hand, encouraging folks to take a journey and then leading the way. So when the owner of this seaside house (*above*) has a barbecue, she knows half her guests are going to end up in the garden, with only her split-rail fence to blame. In fact, the garden has become such a popular party destination that the food is often served under the old grape arbor. Mowed grass paths are extra wide to encourage strolling side by side. When the sun is high in the sky, the flowers look bright as crayons. But the owner of the house insists the garden looks best in the late afternoon, when the fence throws its shadow across the lawn, and the flowers sit in calm anticipation of their nightly watering.

◆ Here in New England, rocky soil is a given; gardeners have to make the best of it. The hillside garden (*above*) is laid out in several well-defined beds. When boulders cropped up and couldn't be easily moved, they were incorporated into the landscape. Prostrate junipers, day lilies and annual flowers planted around the rocks look as though they sprang up naturally. This particular bed of rocks and flowers is ringed by a border of nasturtiums, petunias and lavender.

fence is the classic choice for creating a rustic effect. People who own Colonial homes should consider adding a picket fence to the grounds.

Pergolas can substitute for walls, hedges and fences in defining areas of a yard. You can make your pergola especially appealing by training roses and other gorgeous plants on it. This creates a particularly lovely spot under which to dine. Trellis and lattice enclosures are also options, and have figured prominently in the definition of outdoor rooms for centuries. In the West we think of milled wood slats or pieces of lattice stapled or nailed together. In the East, bamboo is the choice, bound at the joints with a variety of twine such as raffia, hemp or sisal. As a raw design concept, these materials are endlessly useful in developing creature comforts and in providing a place to train desirable but rambling plants so that they take on architectural significance.

Trellising may serve as a dividing wall or fence, as screening for privacy and as a device to frame vistas. It is often applied to the wall of a house in a trompe l'oeil effect, or as an embellishment to wood, concrete or other surfaces that may serve as enclosures. The medium readily extends to arbors, pergolas and summerhouses, affording cohesiveness in the landscape and visual delights in all seasons.

◆ An old greenhouse was sited here (*left*). Instead of demolishing it, the family who lives in this French grange decided to keep the skeletal structure intact. These days, the area is a gardenlike place for dining. The roof of red roses overhead softly filters the sunlight. For this lunch for eight, an outsize bouquet of roses and grapevines presides over the linen-covered table (*above*).

◆ Images from a garden party: A separate table set parallel to the dining table displays a light midday meal, served buffet-style (*top*). It begins, appropriately enough, with fruit of the vine. (The house is in the midst of wine country.) Local cheeses and crudités fresh from the garden are part of summer's bounty. Sun-ripened peaches from orchards on the property make a delectable dessert (*below, right*). Other special touches are provided by pretty tableware and accessories (*below, left*).

◆ To reach the pergola, visitors stroll down a grass path edged with lively perennial borders designed in shades of blue and pink (*opposite*). Inside the pergola is the old stone trough that serves as a base for the dining table.

◆ A garden is an ideal place to incorporate an element of surprise. Example: the terra-cotta urn that nods to one side, behind the bushes in this Maine garden (*opposite and above*). Unexpected, unusual and enticing in its posture, the tilted urn is one of the many delights of this well-scrubbed parcel of land. "It always gets people talking," says the owner of the property. The urn is a cornerstone of sorts for another of the yard's little delights: a sunken living room, alfresco style. The yard used

to drop away precariously here. Now it's terraced and shored up by a stone wall. Two steps in the wall lead visitors down from the main yard. A weathered bench sits in this bosky nook, with foxgloves and planters of sweet peas and peppers for company. Evergreen yews trimmed into fanciful mushroom shapes provide an encircling cushion of privacy, taking over where the stone wall leaves off.

The actual volume of your outdoor space is a major determinant in your design. A large property is usually best handled by breaking it up into several garden areas so that it does not become monotonous. If there is a view beyond the property, this too can play a role in its design. The sight of mountains or a body of water can be dramatized by planting a smooth expanse of manicured lawn leading up to it.

Adding focal points and interesting garden accessories such as urns, statuary, benches and birdbaths leads the eye rhythmically around and brings an aura of liveliness and drama to the garden. If you prefer to keep your garden looking uncomplicated and pristine, consider using rocks as accessories. This creates visual diversity while preserving a romantically naturalistic landscape. Selectively placed pillarlike rocks or boulders take on sculptural qualities in the landscape.

Another visual trick for diversifying a yard is to create different patterns on the ground. A simple design of intersecting knots in an herb garden sketches a serpentine pattern on the ground that makes even a small space eye-catching. The same type of effect can be achieved using paving materials. Brick or stone paths can meander throughout the garden or they can form a radiating pattern leading up to a central feature, such as a birdbath, sundial or sculpture.

◆ A yard can incorporate several outdoor rooms, each with its own style and purpose. Numerous French doors provide access to the yard of this new home in Connecticut, designed by Rob Rye and George Schneider. Terracing tamed the sloping property into a series of manageable levels. Surrounded by a low stone wall typical of the area, a brick patio on the same level as the house (*above*) is decorated with containers of flowering plants and edged with flower beds. Removing many of the old stone walls was the first step in terracing the property. Foxgloves, irises and a mix of annuals line a brick path leading to a pergola in another part of the garden (*opposite*).

BRINGING THE OUTDOORS IN

The backyard has always been central to our lives. Whether we use it most to entertain, to exercise or to relax, the outdoor room is more than an adjunct to the home: It is a vital area whose many functions simply cannot be duplicated within the home. It is a Mediterranean tradition to take meals outdoors and use the yard as frequently as any other well-trafficked interior room, with the difference that it's reserved for pleasure alone. To encourage use of the backyard, it helps to create a graceful and inviting transition from within the home to its exterior.

The materials used in the room are essential to the success of this endeavor. A flooring material such as flagstone or brick that easily makes the transition from indoors to out is a good starting point. Also important is the view to the outdoors. Who could resist stepping out into the garden when double French doors gracefully lead into it? Either left bare or dressed only in the gauziest curtains or lace to let the sun stream through, large glass doors or oversize windows entice us out of the house and into the garden. An air of comfort and familiarity is an essential ingredient in this scenario. Near the windows and doors, items associated with an outdoor life-style can be displayed. Straw hats, baskets, old-fashioned gardening tools, framed antique seed packets and botanical prints and flower arrangements brimming with fresh blossoms from the cutting garden are among the homey, irresistible items that suggest the natural delights that await you outdoors.

◆ This old farmhouse sits empty most days. Why? Because everyone's enjoying the out-of-doors. The pleasant climate and toasting sun are a constant lure. The terrace (*opposite, far left*) is the best place to enjoy it all, sitting at one of a pair of lacy wrought-iron tables. In the house, French doors are left open to invite outdoor lounging. Because the house is large and might appear to be imposing, the owners made a special effort to decorate it in a simple way, both inside and out. This not only suits their barefoot life-style and makes the home welcoming to guests, but it also shows off the "good bones" of each room—arched door-ways, deep-silled casement windows and beamed ceilings. The wicker table and matching club chairs in the sitting room (*opposite, near left*) seem to be a favorite gathering place for people—and their possessions—as they head in and out. Straw chapeaux cluster on the old hat stand near the door, ready to do duty as sunbonnets outside. The sparkling kitchen (*right*) also serves as a pleasurable vantage point from which to enjoy the landscape beyond.

◆ Almost any area of a property can be borrowed for casual entertaining. A simple wicker table, covered with a pair of cotton runners (*left*) is an enticing spot for a summer evening meal. Food that can be prepared in advance, like these salads, is ideal for relaxed outdoor meals.

◆ In warmer climates, the division between indoors and out often becomes indistinct, as living moves easily between house and yard and back again. The pool frequently becomes a focal point for entertaining and relaxing, and access to and from the house should be simple and direct. Sliding glass doors open on to this Florida patio (*left, below*) and draw welcome breezes into the house during warm weather.

◆ A bright floral tablecloth is a perfect way to add color to an alfresco afternoon tea (*opposite*). Simple white slat chairs, which can be folded and stored easily, are gathered around this tea table in Litchfield County, Connecticut. Behind, cosmos, sweet-scented stocks and impatiens create a red, white and pink backdrop.

CHAPTER TWO

ENTRANCES

S ometime after she'd passed the milestone of her ninetieth birthday, Harriet Morse, author of a modern-day classic book, *Gardening in the Shade*, shared her secret of a long life filled with health and happiness: "I look at every person I encounter and say or think with all my might, 'I wish you well.'" The philosophy expressed in those four short words applies directly to the entrance to a property that says, "Welcome home." To all who come calling, the entrance should extend a friendly gesture while also maintaining dignity, reserve and as much security as is appropriate.

The entrance of a house is usually the first glimpse we catch of the heart of the home that lies within. Whether grand or small, formal or informal, this first impression sets the stage for everything else. It should reflect the tone and style of the property it precedes, and it should complement the architecture of the house and the mood of the surrounding landscape. A rustic fence or stone wall, for example, is more at home with an older property; larger properties often call for grander treatments using trees and more emphatic statements in the outdoor room. In small yards, entrance designs are often straightforward and consist of structural devices such as walls and gates. Larger properties present opportunities for dramatic entrances, such as winding driveways leading through woodlands or straight drives framed by sculpted shrubbery directing visitors to the front door.

Garden designer Harland J. Hand, writing in *Garden Design* magazine, notes three essential elements: "Shelter, which gives a feeling of peace and relaxation; a trail, which gives a sense of direction and adventure; and a lookout, a place with a view, which gives a feeling of power and control." All these are possible in the entry garden or outdoor room that says welcome.

◆ A marvelous example of front-yard fundamentals (*previous page*): a couple of easygoing chairs, a chorus line of pansies and thick, cool green grass . . . all set in the shade of a grand old tree. The only hint of the sophisticated gardens beyond is found in twin corkscrew topiaries beside the front door.

◆ One of the charms of the American countryside is its easy, rambling roads. But in many areas there are no signposts, and homeowners have marked their drives with personalized directionals (*opposite*).

All too often when we take over a property we follow somewhat blindly in the steps of those who have gone before us. It's possible to completely rethink how each part of the landscape might best be used to enhance your use of the space. What may have been perceived as a public space—only to be seen from the street and briefly experienced as you and visitors walk from car to door—may be ideally reorganized into an outdoor living room. While such thoughts might seem radical at first, in practice they needn't be. The idea might be to take advantage of mature trees already in place, to transplant foundation plantings so they become screens for privacy or create enticing green vistas when viewed from indoors.

Most homeowners consider a clearly legible house number, displayed either on the home or on a mailbox, a top priority, with visibility at night or in the heaviest downpour being an important provision. In addition to a house number, you may wish to alert your guests to their arrival at your home by clearly displaying your family name on a decorative plaque. This is especially important if your house is set back from the road and not visible through trees. Parking accommodations, either on or off the street, come next. Safety is the operative word in planning the driveway and its access to and from the street or road; this consideration is as important in the country as in urban areas.

◆ From the crest of the hill, the delighted traveler catches a first glimpse of an old stone house located in the Delaware Valley (*above*). A path of local stone sweeps toward the house, flanked by lightly trimmed hedges of boxwood. Both the hedges and the ivy that climbs the house bring year-round color to the property.

◆ New Englanders are justly famous for their thrift. A case in point: This old well-sweep (*opposite*), which has a new role as a roadside signpost. The gardens are planted in a few large beds, which begin at the grape arbor near the house and then cascade down the hill. Residents of the garden (*clockwise, from above*) include masses of mid-century 'Enchantment' lilies clustered in groups, dahlias and delphiniums hugging the fence, and roses like 'Perfume Delight' selected for fragrance.

◆ Depending on its style, a fence sets the tone for a property. A fence is used to define outdoor areas, whether they are intimate gardens or wide, open spaces. At the beach (*opposite, above*), not much separates the brick patio from the shifting sands except for these paddocklike barriers. An old wood cask has been planted with sun-loving geraniums. On a smaller property, orange day lilies cluster around a white picket fence (*opposite, below*), waving their joyous heads. The simple English-style fence (*above*) is a perfect anchor for a garden of cottage blooms, including cosmos and phlox in pink and white.

From the classic white picket fence, which conjures up fond images of the traditional American town, to the more formidable barrier of a high brick wall, the fence also helps to establish the first impression of a property. Open fences—post-and-rail, picket or railings—clearly establish a boundary without enclosing a property. Vines and spreading creepers like wisteria and clematis or thickly planted flower beds will soften the linear quality of open fences with their exuberant growth. Brick walls, board fences and other solid barriers are more imposing and intriguing at the same time, as we are drawn to discover the secrets they enclose. Where privacy or security is important, a solid barrier or fence is most effective, but these can have the effect of making a property look smaller, especially if it is already quite modest. Solid boundaries, especially high walls, will shelter the property from the worst of winter winds and create protective microclimates within their confines. More tender plants will flourish in the warmth of a south-facing wall, and the growing season will be extended as warm air is held in the garden.

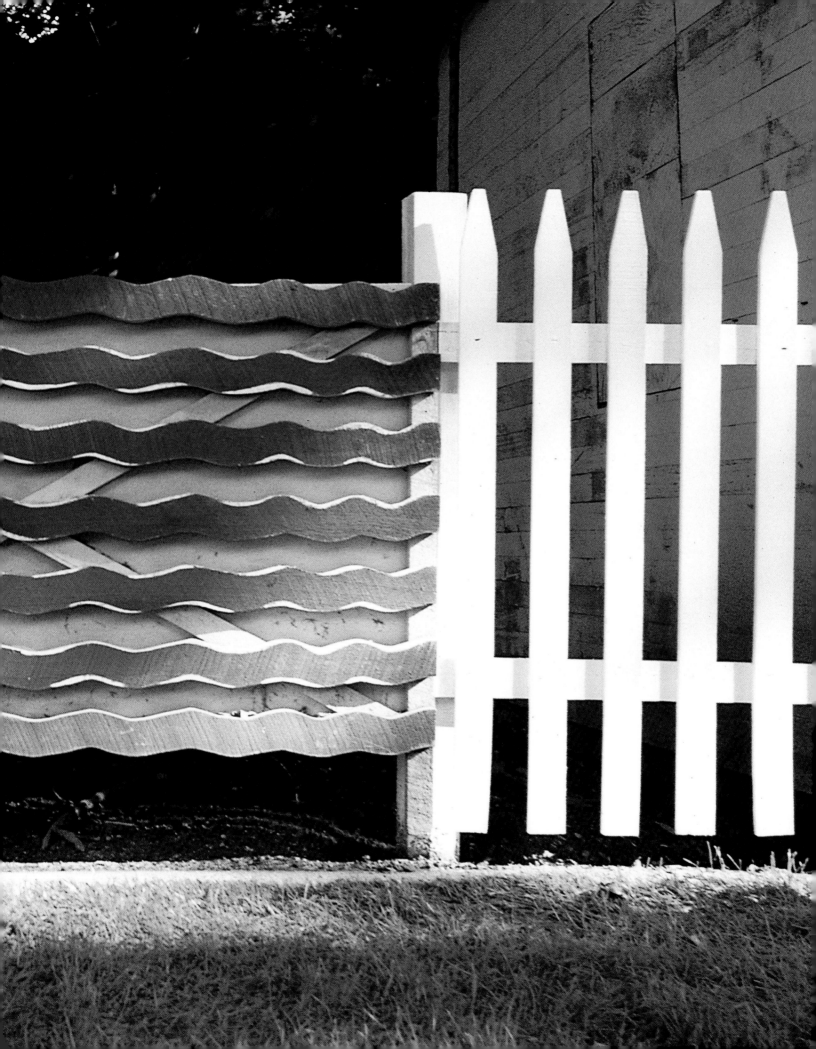

◆ Old Glory waves a patriotic greeting from the gate of designer Mary Emmerling's country house (*previous page*). This folk art re-creation of the flag has wavy "stripes," so it seems as though it is flying in the wind.

◆ Stone steps lead down to a geometric garden gate of wood and chicken wire (*above*) that attempts to keep the neighborhood groundhog at bay. The effect is picturesque, the gate laden with tumbling passion vines and ivy.

The garden gate is the quintessential greeting device on a property. It is instrumental in creating a first impression, and its style should embody the message you wish to convey. Gates should take their scale and style from the surrounding boundary fence—solid and formidable or open and welcoming. A solid high gate makes an emphatic statement and discourages casual visitors. It also serves a very practical purpose, offering greater security and privacy to the homeowner. High gates also foster a sense of drama and formality. Low, open gates imply a freedom to come and go as one pleases. The material from which a gate is constructed not only sets a tone—wood is usually casual and inviting, metal tends to be more stately and imposing—but also must be in keeping with the architecture of the house and the style of the garden.

Gates are important transitional devices on a property, as they allow entrances and exits through hedges, fences and walls. They may restrain small children and house pets, but in the main gates serve the symbolic

◆ Twin arching yews join hands above the entrance to a Nantucket yard (*above*). The hand-painted gate between the hedges, embellished with holly-hocks, extends a cheer-ful welcome.

design functions of framing a scene and giving what lies beyond a sense of mystery.

Gates in general can be greatly enhanced by the additional framing device of an arbor or archway, the latter achieved through construction or by the careful training and shearing in season of a tall, living hedge such as yew, privet, ficus or whatever plant is locally adapted and whose growth can be shaped to the purpose. This is a traditional practice in European gardens. Constructed arbors of metal, wood or bamboo invite the establishment on either side of favorite vines and climbers. Popular choices include honeysuckle, wisteria, jasmine, climbing roses intertwined with clematis and, among quick-from-seed annuals, morning glory, moonvine, scarlet runner and hyacinth beans.

Another way to emphasize a gate is to flank it with large, matching terra-cotta pots or other planters, or garden statuary such as *couchant* dogs, lions or sphinxes. If the gate opens inward, arrange these objects outside, or vice versa.

CREATING A PATH

Once through a gate, we look to pathways to guide our movements throughout the yard. Paths not only lead the visitor from place to place, but also divide different garden areas from one another. Fences and walls can serve this purpose, but paths are a more subtle way of marking boundaries because they are an integral part of the ground plane. The simplest of paths leads directly from the edge of the property to the front door. If the property has a formal tone, such a path might be edged by a line of trimmed evergreens, a border of perennials and herbs or even a low dry-stone wall. Concrete and brick are excellent choices for such paths. Straight lines belong most on formal properties, where paths and patios as well as trees and plants are ordered, much as in classic garden design.

Meandering pathways are better suited to natural-looking landscapes. A property with wooded or hilly areas is complemented by a path leading circuitously through it, snaking around rocks and trees and perhaps even connecting with a bridge over a small stream. Allow plantings to spill over the edges of the path and even become so overgrown that they obscure what lies beyond the next bend. On less formal properties the path can be paved with gravel, flagstone or local stone, with hardy low-growing plants growing up between its crevices. If these are fragrant varieties like the herbs thyme, lavender or rosemary, then guests will be welcomed with their sweet scents. The stepping-stone path is an appropriate choice for a Japanese-style garden, but it is also at home in the informal

yard. Pathways need not be paved at all and can simply consist of bare earth, which creates a nice effect in the woodland garden.

Throughout the property, paths can continue in the same materials or change to signify the transition between areas, between the front door and a garden path, for example, or from a garden path to a wooded area. Paths leading through flower gardens allow you to stroll through and enjoy their fragrance. Within the herb or vegetable plot, pathways are extremely practical features. They allow the gardener easy access for weeding the plots and harvesting. Paths within gardens that need constant upkeep should be wide enough to accommodate a wheelbarrow.

◆ Two views of a garden that demonstrates the fine art of creating a dramatic entry (*opposite, left and right*): Beyond the rustic twig gate set beneath a privet hedge arch, a flagstone terrace welcomes the visitor. Within, a brick path glides through the garden, past tubs of tuberous begonias, to a twin hedge that leads in turn to the glorious cutting garden.

◆ In a tiny city garden, everything seems richer, more intense. The stone footpath (*above, left*) that approaches the conservatory is necessarily narrow, to give further territory to the plants. At a crossroads in the garden (*above, right*), a reading seat has been placed between a tub of colorful petunias, geraniums and ivy and another of trimmed evergreen boxwood.

◆ In the barren front yard of a newly moved house in Connecticut, garden designer Paul Sakren created a fast-growing cottage garden (*above*). Against the teal-blue house, Sakren used a palette (*left*) that ranged from indigo to ruby red, complemented by clear pinks. Fresh-cut flowers gathered from his new garden (*opposite*) include pink and purple cosmos, phlox and delphiniums.

◆ Tall, slender trees serve as a sculptural buffer for the old French farmhouse set in the clearing beyond them (*above*). Over the years, the house has settled into its surroundings, the natural tones of its gray roof, green shutters and timeworn bricks melding with the encircling foliage of evergreen and deciduous trees. Even the old woodie looks as though it might have been paneled with lumber from the log pile in front.

◆ Flowers and open doors and windows: That's how the people in tiny French towns traditionally welcome friends. At the old farmhouse (*right*), giant sunflowers post their welcome from the windowsill. Neighbors going to market often linger here to talk about the morning's news, with a bank of lavender hydrangeas, mustard-yellow nasturtiums and silver lace blooming at their feet. Above the front door, a utilitarian light epitomizes the no-nonsense country style.

◆ Flowers can soften a vista, color a yard and create a warm welcome anywhere. When this color is played against that of the house, the results are enchanting. In the side yard of florist Ken Turner's London house (*opposite*), the profusion of geraniums in the most intense shades of red, orange and magenta is a foil for the soft pink walls.

◆ In tropical climates (*above, left*), the houses bloom with color right along with the flowers. Here, a pale pink stucco house with soft blue shutters is framed by bougainvillea vines and underscored by bright-red impatiens that cluster along the sidewalk. A tree came down in the front yard of this 1800s house in Michigan (*above, right*), but the empty space was quickly taken up by a bright batch of cosmos.

◆ In the ultramodern entryway (*opposite*) to a Long Island, New York, house, a bold swivel door has a slice-of-glass window. Its look is a fitting indication of the house's dramatic interior and is a distinct contrast to the traditional white shingles that mark the exterior of the house, which was designed by architect Bruce Nagel. Planked decking outside the door was stained a pale-blue and the curving wall painted pink to flow continuously from outdoors to in. Gray tiles in the foyer were chosen for their practicality as well as for their graphic good looks.

◆ A pediment is the friendly cap that finishes off a doorway. For this house (*above, left*), fishtail shingles on the pediment give an interesting aspect to what would otherwise be just a long stretch of clapboard. Oddball squashes grown in the garden are set here after harvesting and make a colorful statement at the foot of simple steps.

◆ To make a portico more than just a covered entryway, the framework of a classical structure was sheathed in latticework at this home in Atlanta, Georgia (*above, right*). The lattice softens the formality of the portico's tall columns and fanlike pediment and suits its casual setting as a bridge between the brick patio and the front door up the steps.

Inviting or imposing, classic or casual, dramatic or unassuming, the front door can send a message to a visitor as clearly as any other element of the entrance garden. Think of the welcoming sense of ease that an entrance with only a screen door conveys to a guest, or the considerate attention to detail that a front door with etched- or stained-glass insets depicting a cheerful scene brings to an entryway.

Lighting around the front door is both a practical necessity and a signal of welcome to guests on a dark night. Wall-mounted fixtures are usually sufficient and should provide a warm glow over any front steps.

If the entrance is to be informal, continuing the same kinds of materials from outside to the entrance or hall—tile, brick or wood—creates a blending between indoors and out and enhances a casual tone. Halls and breezeways can also ease the transition between outdoors and in. The home with a porch, small portico or sheltered entrance is more practical for inclement weather and, at the same time, benefits from this transitional indoor-outdoor space.

Decorating the area around the front door with seasonal touches, such as autumnal gourds and festive holiday wreaths, makes visitors immediately feel wel-

come and beautifies the entryway. The same ornaments can be continued as a decorative theme within the foyer, further uniting the indoors and outdoors.

Screen doors, large windows and glass doors further mute the boundaries of home and garden, bringing the pleasures of the outdoors inside. Allowing the garden to grow right up to the front door or planting a favorite tree in sight of French windows further adds to our appreciation of the yard when we are indoors. Flowers that release their fragrance in the evening planted beneath a bedroom window—certain sweet-scented stocks, jasmines, honeysuckles and evening primroses, for example—will perfume the air on a summer night. Similarly, a front door shrouded by the heavy blooms of climbing roses or a wisteria vine entwined around a trellis is a romantic and irresistible entrance, a place where the garden seems to have reached right up to the house to say "welcome."

If your home is on an acre or more, there is the possibility, if not the necessity, of an extended driveway. Whether the driveway is curved or straight, formal or informal, surface treatments and plantings on either side are both useful and attractive. In fact, hardly any plantings offer as much potential for grandness and drama as an *allée* of trees. These may be evergreen or deciduous, slow- or fast-growing. Avoid trees having brittle wood or large surface roots.

◆ Rather than tucking the garages into an unseen corner of their property, the owners of this house set them prominently in the front yard and gave them bold blue doors (*above*), as well as their own postmodern frame of red cedar. Practical for car and boat storage, the two garages form an entranceway that leads through a white gravel courtyard to the main door. The rambling house, with a third story that captures a view of the sea miles away, was designed by architect Oliver Cope. The trim around all the windows and doors is punctuated by snappy white paint, customary in New England shingle-style houses. A splash of turquoise accents the arching door (*right*) that opens to a second-story study. On the walkway outside the door, a pot brims with impatiens that stays in bloom from early spring to the first frost of autumn.

◆ In European gardens, walks and pathways have evolved over the centuries. One of the most popular is of white gravel: It is bright, discourages weeds, and it gently echoes the contours of the garden. In this yard (*above, left and right*), a borderless path proceeds apace past a rose hedge and barns, then gracefully curves to wrap around the house. From within (*opposite*), the path gradually fades from sight.

In a rural setting, it is often possible to organize the access road to a house so that one approaches by driving past or through a field, meadow, pasture or woodland. If along the way the journey involves crossing a bridge and stream, or even over the utilitarian cattle guard, the transition from outer world to private domain is underscored.

Driveways, garages and entrance courts usually involve paved surfaces. The wetter the climate, the greater the need for a covered port of arrival. Where street parking is not permissible, or it is possible to avoid, find room on the property for parking two or three cars. If heavy snowfall is a possibility, a place will be needed for piling up snow as the plow comes through.

Designing an attractive entrance that serves both practical and aesthetic needs is one of the most rewarding aspects of creating an outdoor space. It involves planning and forethought, but the results are well worth the effort. The entrance area of your property should convey your style as fully as does your interior design. The way it is structured and organized, as well as the way visitors use and respond to it, may change over time. But this is all part of the continual evolution of the outdoor room. Its design should be strong enough to direct people through it, yet flexible enough to change with a family's needs.

◆ Sometimes the best-looking gardens are a result of letting Nature have her way. Witness the greenery that overruns this French entrance (*left*). Clematis covering the putty-colored walls hints at years of unchecked growth, all the more luxuriant because of the neglect. Pretty pink hollyhocks tap their slender branches on the panes of the tall white window and an open door. From inside looking out (*right, above*), the writing desk has a view of trees and the garden. On the desk, a tall crystal jug of roses, foxgloves and lupines (*right, below*) enlivens this corner of the room.

CHAPTER THREE

PORCHES & PATIOS

Few activities are more enticing or refreshing than a summer afternoon of reading on the patio or a lazy afternoon repast in the shade of a porch. Spending time relaxing outdoors is one of our most precious pastimes, and extending the home outdoors is a natural inclination. Porches and patios offer a middle ground between indoors and outdoors. These spaces are designed to give us pleasure from simply being outdoors.

The porch tends to be a gathering place with an old-fashioned charm that comes partly from open-air informality and easygoing style. Made instantly companionable by its captured breezes and dappled sun, the porch is poised on the boundary between the solidity of the house and the freedom of the outdoors. Across America it appears in countless forms and variations, ranging from the Victorian gingerbread confections of Cape May, New Jersey, to the simple verandas of the South, to the classic porches of the New England coast, oriented to take in a view of the sea.

Patios, open to the elements, provide an even more direct entrée to nature than the porch. It is not unusual to find them equipped with a barbecue and a simply designed picnic table, making them nonpareil settings for informal meals. The patio dovetails with many life-styles: Enclosed by a hedge or fence, it becomes a secluded spot; when left open at its perimeter and filled with casual, colorful furniture, it takes on a welcoming, convivial look. Terraces are more formal than patios but are virtually identical in design. They, too, are usually not sheltered by a roof and tend to be long and narrow, sometimes ornamented by a colonnade.

Whether these outdoor rooms are filled with furniture, plants or both, the challenge for their inhabitants is to personalize the area with the objects that make them feel most comfortable. The only decorating rule is to achieve a harmony with the house itself.

◆ A lushly draped wrap-around porch (*previous page*) is outfitted in exotic blue-and-white cotton. Fresh white wicker furniture suits the indoor-outdoor mood. Beyond the railing, a living wall of evergreens surrounds the porch and its grass court for privacy. Pots of shade-loving, red-and-pink begonias and gloxinias inject warmer colors into the cool palette.

◆ For a new shingle-style cottage in Southampton, New York (*opposite*), architect James Volney Righter designed an expansive porch that takes in the view of the gardens and pond beyond. On another property (*above*), the owners use a curving terrace overlooking a lake as a second dining room during all but the very coldest months of the year. Its perch among the treetops affords a wide-open perspective. A reinforced canvas awning lashed overhead shields diners from the sun.

Whatever term best describes an outdoor living area, convention should not dictate its decoration and design. Because it is not part of the house proper, a porch or terrace can benefit from a less deliberate, more whimsical decorating hand. Effects that might seem inappropriate or even outrageous indoors—fabric-covered ceilings, exceptionally mismatched furniture, boldly painted floors—flourish in this more relaxed environment. Nature may insinuate herself indirectly into the design of these outdoor spaces—in pots of flowering plants, trellises of morning glory or on the pattern of a tablecloth.

Color plays such a central role in determining the look of an environment, and the ways that people react to it, that it should be one of the first considerations in decorating an outdoor room. It is one of the easiest ways of completely transforming a space. Quick color changes keep the porch in harmony with the seasons. Fabrics in cooling blue shades or covered with bright floral patterns are appropriate for warm-weather months; richer, earthier fabric colors complement changing foliage in autumn. In general, the stronger the degree of sunlight streaming into an area, the more successful vivid, stand-out colors will be. Strong light dilutes our perception of color.

Therefore, light-drenched environments need hues that can stand up to the sun. Tropical, southern and southwestern porches, patios and terraces benefit from a bright dose of color in furniture and fabrics. Neutral colors or white on the floors and ceilings, overhangs or canopies allow the bright tones of furnishings to emerge. Another option is to weave brilliant strands of color throughout, enlivening everything with their presence. This applies as much to pillows, curtains, tablecloths and other soft furnishings as it does to chairs, tables and accessories. The primary colors of a bright blue wicker table, a pretty red vase and a cheerful yellow birdcage all have tremendous color impact in a room when color is otherwise used sparingly.

Because porches and terraces lead directly off the house, colors and furnishings indoors and out should blend and harmonize, minimizing the transition. The outdoor area will, of course, take some of its color and mood from the surrounding garden and views. Robustly colored flowers such as hibiscus, clematis and dahlias, and lush green leaves twined around railings or a trellis, will also contribute color to the porch. Porches, patios and terraces are also the ideal places to nurture container plants. Even the smallest flowers will receive the close attention they need, and several containers form a portable garden that can be grouped together to add impact to an evening dinner party or spread out for larger gatherings.

◆ What's a porch without pillows? They invite relaxation, especially when those pillows are covered in chintz. For years, chintz pillows have been a tradition on porches. They're like botanical prints, bringing the lushness and detail of flowers up close for lasting enjoyment. On a screened porch (*right*), the tumble of florals on a love seat looks right at home with the basketful of lilies of the valley that are the signature of spring.

◆ A rustic log-legged table set with a cheerful cloth (*left and opposite*) is the focus for relaxed outdoor meals set out under an old shade tree at the house of French designer Bernard Perris. Diners choose their chairs from the array scattered about the flagstone-and-gravel patios. Teal wicker and deep-blue dishes echo the colors of sea and sky. Cachepots on the table hold early summer flowers—peonies and roses, foxgloves and hydrangeas—put together by Perris with artless elegance. From the table, guests can take in a view of the well-tended gardens or the old stone house.

ENTERTAINING OUTDOORS

Early-morning sun or candlelit meals alfresco have an irresistible charm and pleasure that stimulate the palate and enhance any gathering. Conversation is relaxed, the meal is comfortable and informal and even the simplest salad and the humblest bread take on a special quality in the fresh air. At night, a candlelit porch or patio takes on a magical quality. In many parts of France and Italy meals outside under the shade of trees is a natural and ancient way of life. Protected by a hedge or a screen, a sun-washed outdoor dining area can be sheltered enough to enjoy in all but the coldest months.

The key to successful outdoor dining is informality—plates can be simple and even mismatched, linens colorful, guests should feel free to come and go as they please. Outdoors few rules apply. Containers filled with flowers in a range of hues can be moved around the outdoor dining room to inject color. Favorite scented plants—lavender, thyme, sweet pea—can be planted close by to perfume the area used for entertaining.

◆ The terrace of a stone house has a built-in plus: The exterior stone walls of the house become an inviting backdrop for all that goes on outside. Designer John Saladino pointed up the facade of his country boathouse (*above*) by extending its rustic flavor to his terrace. Here, the watchwords are comfort and ease. Canvas market umbrellas tilt in the sunshine, casting shade over twin tables set for an early lunch. Simple wire garden chairs are "bathrobed" in white terry cloth slipcovers—great seating for those who've just returned from a sail or swim. Tables are covered in fresh raspberry bandbox-striped cotton. The floral centerpieces reflect Saladino's penchant for combining country elements with sophistication: in this case, city-bought roses with garden sweet peas and delphiniums.

◆ A shaded overhang is an ideal place to set up a dining table. In fact, once the ideal spot for outdoor dining is found, there's no need to move the table again. That's the reason the owners of this house (*right*) built a table in a permanent spot on their terrace, surrounding the festive columns that support the roof above. Utterly taken with the soft light of the terrace and its closeness to their gardens, they found their guests lingered here naturally, just as they did in the kitchen in winter. During summer weekends, the terrace table is set with foods arranged buffet style, so friends and family can eat whenever they please. And because the house is in France, the staples of every feast are always fresh fruit, cheese and a selection of breads just brought in from the market in town. Jugs of wine cool in the shadow of what was once a working brick oven. Bouquets from the cutting garden decorate the wood table, bleached by years of benevolent sunshine.

◆ Dressed in full summer splendor (*opposite*), the porch becomes another full-fledged room of the house. The "bones" of the porch couldn't be simpler: an old-fashioned board-and-batten ceiling, classic columns, a slatted porch railing. The allure is in the trimmings, here by designer Ron Grimaldi. Swagged shades are loaded with fringe, chairs are cushioned with Rose Cumming chintz in a grape pattern, and ivy climbs a table skirt fresh as a ballgown. Not a single detail has been overlooked: the ceiling light with ruffled shade, the well-placed fan, flowers spilling from majolica vases, and potted palms and rose bushes to bring the outdoors even nearer. At the end of the room, candles are lit at dusk.

◆ Crisp latticework provides a measure of shade for a tranquil porch (*above*) designed by Tonin Mac Callum. The house itself has been painted buttery yellow and the sisal floor covering is camel colored—two hues that bring warmth when the sun has passed. Set amid the greenery is a porch necessity: a comfortable rocking chair.

The porch is arguably the most versatile room in the house. It acts as an indoor-outdoor space that can serve many needs—whether they are entertaining, gardening in containers or simply relaxation.

The American porch is undergoing a renaissance after decades of indifference to its charms. Although it is traditionally the place where families gather and lovers pop the question, the porch lost its place of importance for a time in recent American history. Now, at the end of the twentieth century, a renewed appreciation for vernacular architecture has beckoned people to take a seat on the porch swing once again.

The little touches that decorate the porch are every bit as vital as the furniture. The wall connected to the house is a perfect place to display cherished antiques such as an old baker's rack entwined with cascades of vines and seasonal flowers, or to set up a service bar. Unadorned porch walls invite hanging wreaths fashioned from grapevine, bittersweet, honeysuckle or evergreen clippings as well as dried flowers, treasures picked up from nature walks or such conversation pieces as old garden tools, baskets and straw hats. Folksy ornaments such as ship figureheads and cigar-store Indians bring a lively air to the porch.

Most people's dream porches are airy and provide direct contact with nature on balmy summer days and nights. But porches that are cozy during inclement weather and are free from insects are also welcoming places to sit and relax. Of course, no porch can provide such amenities without careful planning by its owners.

An enclosed porch serves its owners year-round, offering comfort and shelter in the midst of January's blustery days, or a protected place to listen to a heavy spring rainstorm. Large, interchangeable storm windows and screens, often found in older houses, make the porch a secure stage from which the season's changes in the garden and weather can be enjoyed.

But perhaps what makes a porch feel most like a room is how it is decorated. The most successful porches—meaning the most lived-in—have commodious furniture, at once comfortable and durable. A great sentimental favorite, a porch swing can be situated to take advantage of views and invite use while also not bumping into other furnishings. There are also freestanding porch swings, gliders and a variety of hammocks for indulging in delicious laziness. Wicker, plain wood and twig rocking chairs are also wonderful choices for the porch.

◆ The surprise of dark-painted wicker and a spectacular stenciled floor (*previous page*) are a winning combination for this huge porch, canopied each spring for warm-weather use. The owners wanted furniture kept to a minimum in order to best show off the floor. Designer Gary Crain has chosen a play of patterns that gives an upbeat tempo to the mix of pillows, tablecloths and chair cushions.

◆ The simple appeal of this romantic veranda (*above*) begins underfoot. Instead of rugs, sun casts striped shadows across the painted floor. The owners blended two sets of unmatched white wicker into a congenial grouping and cushioned all the pieces with blue cotton patterned

with tiny hearts. The hearts seem to echo the curlicued shapes of the more elaborate love seat and chair. Suspended above the porch railing, petunias in hanging baskets form a flowering cornice that perfumes the air and frames the view of the lawn beyond.

◆ Interior designer Bunny Williams imbued client Pam Kay's home with a fresh yet timeless look. This simply furnished porch with floor-to-ceiling screens (*opposite*) is so at one with nature, it's hard to tell where "indoors" ends and the real outdoors begins. The herringbone-patterned brick floor and weathered wood harmonize beautifully with pillows in soft gray and pink shades.

◆ The grace of nineteenth-century living is evoked on this porch in upstate New York (*opposite*). Commodious wicker seating sets a casual tone, complemented by basketry and occasional tables, which are scattered around the porch.

◆ Devoted gardeners live here, and it shows (*above*). The backyard hedge separating this property from the neighbors' is softened by a thriving cutting garden that stays in bloom from early spring to the final days of fall. The accumulation of garden paraphernalia that always ends up on the back porch forms a still life of sorts, representative of the daily work that goes on here to keep the property in top form. Shaded by latticework, a potting table is set just inside the porch, so it's easy to arrange flowers into natural bouquets just as soon as they're picked.

◆ A basic picket fence is the all-American frame for a circa 1894 home in Key West (*left*). In this town, porches are as pervasive as the bougainvillea—and just as brilliantly colored. And the clear, strong sunlight intensifies the effect. Witness the difference the change of light has on the second-story porch (*above*). During the shady morning hours here, a quartet of white wicker is a suitable place for enjoying coffee or for bird-watching. At day's end, the flag is folded and the porch becomes a platform for watching the sun go down.

Although there are surely exceptions, porch architecture is usually most successful if it complements the style of the main building. If a dwelling does not even have a stoop around which a porch can be built, an architect can help add a porch in keeping with a home's architectural style. Front porches, like front gardens, are often more formal than side porches, which tend to resemble family rooms. Back porches may be purely serviceable or private retreats, for everything from sleeping to changing babies to shelling peas and arranging flowers. The style of any porch, however, is a completely personal decision.

Porches do not have to be located on the first level of a home. Second- and upper-story porches, sited to take advantage of marvelous views, are popular architectural features in warm climates, where snow accumulation on the porch floor is not a problem. In such cases, porches with all sides open to the elements—shielded only by a roof for protection from rain—are appropriate, since they allow cooling breezes to enter from all sides and do not restrict views. It is usually more of an undertaking to add a porch to an upper story of a home than it is to build one on ground level. One possibility is to add one on top of a flat garage roof. Another solution is to create an extension to the home, in keeping with its architecture, and locate the porch on top. This area could act as guest sleeping quarters, and doors could open from the bedroom directly onto the porch.

◆ In Seaside, Florida, a planned community on the Gulf of Mexico, access to the outdoors is built in and casual living becomes a way of life. Each house has open-air porches . . . front, side, back, second-story and even rooftop (*above, left*).

◆ The town's master planners chose to imitate the simple, graphic shapes of southern farmhouses, barns and sheds in their designs (*above, right*).

◆ The gulf is known for its spectacular, colorful sunsets (*opposite*). The owner of this house chose to hang twin hammocks from the rafters of his private perch high above the surf. Lights leading to the house are purposely dim, so as not to interfere with late-night stargazing.

Because porches are exposed to the elements for at least part of the year, they must have durable floors. It is common on porches to lay down wide, unfinished planks of such woods as cypress, cedar and redwood. Some people annually give their porch floors a face-lift with battleship-gray deck paint—not a bad idea if that's an appropriate color, but there are lots of options, including silk-screened designs, stencils and patterns in almost any color scheme imaginable. It is easier to maintain a porch floor if it readily sheds rainwater and if it can be swept or even hosed off. Some people opt for porch floor coverings that are impervious to water. Ceiling treatments also set the design tone of a porch. A favorite color—such as blue, which echoes the summer sky and suggests coolness—can be painted on the ceiling. The really ambitious can drape and shirr fabric on the ceiling and the furniture.

Once you have decided on a design scheme for the porch, it is time to fill in the spaces with plants. House-plants too delicate to survive in the outdoors yet in need of fresh air and abundant light enjoy a new lease on life when grown on a porch. Gloxinias, Cape primroses and African violets can't tolerate direct rainwater on their fuzzy leaves, yet in the shelter of a porch they grow and bloom abundantly. Begonias, fuchsias, impatiens, fancy-leaved caladiums and browallias take to the shadier spots, while geraniums, Chinese hibiscus and summer jasmines go for more sun.

Porches are also the ideal places to train a variety of topiaries, tree-form standards and other plants such as Japanese bonsai. While such specimens require great devotion, in practice they yield hours of pleasure from minutes spent here and there, directing their growth. Some popular plants for training include dwarf myrtle, rosemary, and scented geraniums.

◆ In a woodsy setting, sun shouldn't go to waste. This new conservatory (*left*) provides its owners with cozy, year-round "outdoor" dining. Lush, oversize palms echo the property's tall trees, and seasonal color comes from clumps of delphiniums in terra-cotta pots.

◆ The owners of this northern California home carved out two separate places on their property for enjoying the out-of-doors. In keeping with their concept of distinct areas, they've created boundaries between each with great tubs of geraniums and topiaries, and high latticework panels. Close to the house and swimming pool, a patio table surrounded by country twig chairs is shaded by an Italian market umbrella (*opposite and above, left*). The latticed privacy fence, hung with flowering plants and lined with topiary, gives a gazebolike air to the garden setting. Under the boughs of some stately old trees farther afield (*above, right*) a row of topiaries borders a shady seating nook that overlooks Napa Valley vineyards. In a show of unity, the twig furniture wears the same white canvas used on the chairs.

The process of decorating the patio is more flexible than the porch because the boundaries of the area are fluid and open. Unlike the porch, or even the terrace with its enclosed sides, the patio is merely a suggestion of space on the ground plane. It becomes an outdoor room when furniture, containers and most especially company are brought to it.

Because patios are visually associated more with the yard than with the house, they look their best decorated to complement the style of the garden—be it a verdant expanse of lawn, a riotously colored perennial border or a formal tennis court. A patio at a seashore home, for example, lends itself to colors such as sand, aqua and other complementary shades of the ocean.

Some forethought can also make enjoying life on the patio possible under all sorts of weather conditions. Equipping a table with a collapsible umbrella can prevent dinner parties from being ruined by unexpected cloudbursts. The same umbrella will act as a pleasant sun protector on summer afternoons. A gathering of several colorful umbrellas creates a festive air for a brunch and will also shield southward- and westward-oriented patios that receive ample sunshine. Temporary shade from a canvas awning, which can be raised or lowered depending on the occasion, is always a delightful and useful amenity.

◆ Inspired by French Burgundian architecture, this city courtyard in Atlanta, Georgia (*left*), is a world unto itself. Walled in and private, it's a perfect place for entertaining. Two tables make it easy to accommodate almost any kind of gathering. Sometimes there are sit-down suppers. More often, there are big buffets. Long benches are preferred over chairs—they seat more people—but if chairs are the choice, there is a matching pair of wrought-iron seats fashioned in a fern pattern. One sunny wall proved an ideal place to train vines, and after many years the greenery has formed a leafy frame for the handsome double doors leading to the house. The weathered wheelbarrow is an inventive container for flowers; a hearty old rooster welcomes guests at the garden gate.

◆ When the owners of this clapboard house built a poolhouse addition, they took the opportunity to extend their patio (*above*) as well. Airy outdoor furniture is in keeping with the light look of the two-bench arbor that offers a respite from the summer sun. Lush plantings thrive in easy-to-tend elevated beds on either side of the arbor.

◆ American decorator Bill Goldsmith has a way with growing things (*previous page*). On his French country patio, intriguing vignettes are everywhere. Even the spokes of the picnic umbrella (*left*) are put to good use: They're a logical place to hang fresh herbs to dry, and diners are treated to the fragrance of parsley, sage and mint as they eat.

◆ Here, fruits and flowers are all that's needed in the way of decoration. On a rustic old chest that serves as a sideboard (*opposite, clockwise from top left*), pears and oranges keep company with garden blossoms stacked in a casual display. One corner of the still life seems to be just an array of reds: pears and roses on a down-home red-checked napkin. The table needs no formal setting. Garden tools are the "art" on the walls, pebbles the "rug" underfoot, with a nest of brilliant coleus beneath the table in place of firelight. Gardener Goldsmith's strawberry patch is especially fruitful, and these just-picked berries—with blossoms and leaves intact—provide a simple, succulent dessert. Harbingers of summer: dewy, violet-toned hydrangeas.

The patio is a place to mingle natural and structural elements. Although container plants grouped in corners of the patio are a delight to the eye, plantings directly around the patio are equally integral to its atmosphere—a large tree, which provides natural shading, or sweetly scented herbs such as rosemary and lavender, which define the edges of the patio while also imparting delicious environmental fragrance. Ornamental grasses are wonderful to cultivate on a patio's edges as well as in containers. Their soft textures ease the transition from patio to yard.

Patio floors can also be planted with species that are integral to the design. In paved areas, pockets for trees, shrubs, flowers and favorite garden herbs are possible, and spaces between bricks or flagstones can be embellished with such pleasing carpeters as creeping thyme and Corsican mint. Nearby flower gardens might even self-sow tracked or windblown seeds, which will spring up between bricks or stones.

◆ The brick terrace of this country house (*right*) is the essence of simplicity. The warmth of the sun and the fragrance of lavender drift in on the breeze from nearby fields. Though there are no foundation plantings, stone troughs and large terra-cotta pots are filled with a colorful abundance of flowers. Poised alongside the dining room shutters is a pink rose standard (*above*).

◆ A New York City pent-house loft—created and owned by architect Walter Chatham and artist and furniture designer Mary Adams Chatham—spills out to a patio at different levels (*above*). Plantings are necessarily limited to those in containers, which the owners have turned to their advantage by creating portable gardens. At one corner of the patio (*right*), a table and chairs of unfinished wood are warmed with the last of the afternoon sun. In front of a spectacular view of lower Manhattan, the outdoor library is protected from rain with a glass bell (*opposite*).

Patio floors also contribute to the beauty of this outdoor room. Ideally, they should have surfaces that do not create a glare. A nonskid surface is equally vital, especially if there is a pool located nearby or if there are children running about. Practical considerations aside, the surface should harmonize with surrounding architecture and building materials. Bricks are good choices for the patio, fulfilling aesthetic and practical requirements with their nonglare, nonskid qualities. In color and texture, bricks marry with almost any setting, informal or formal. Concrete is easily customized to suit any number of design needs. It can be finished in perfectly smooth or nubby textures and can even be colored to match or contrast with the house and plantings on the property. Tiles come in an even wider range of colors and finishes. Tiles are most effective if they do not have to withstand extended periods of below-freezing temperatures, making them a favorite in warm climates.

For those who prefer free-form or less formal patios, flagstones are a good choice. Their irregular shapes and subtle variations in color can be combined to create a visually intriguing patio floor. Although flagstone is not the smoothest surface, it is worth considering, especially to establish endearing plants in pockets between stones. Creeping thyme, Corsican mint and tufted small perennials such as dianthus and sea pinks all establish themselves nicely on flagstone patios.

◆ In its tropical climate, this patio (*above and right*) comes as a cool surprise. Its architecture is like that of a stage, framed by a classical pediment and columns and flanked by towering palms. The space is a stately foil for the dramatic foliage outside. With the pool just steps away, white built-in seats and a few rattan pieces with bright cotton cushions are purposely no-fuss. When sun and wind threaten to intrude, the floor-length curtain is drawn across the entry to act as a soft enclosure.

◆ At author-gardener Barbara Ohrbach's house, an afternoon's repast always includes fresh-picked vegetables from the garden. And the logical place for cocktails and crudités is the long white porch (*left and above*) with its view of the surrounding hills. Whoever is around at four o'clock—and that might include nieces, nephews and assorted friends—knows to gather on the porch and grab a seat. The garden furniture is left out in all seasons, and it has weathered to a friendly shade of gray. Backs weary from weeding and picking flowers are assuaged by the sturdy plaid pillows placed on every seat.

◆ The mood of an Italian villa is evoked by a brick-paved terrace (*previous page*), bounded by tall white pillars on one side, a decorative railing on the other, and a surrounding brace of trees. The rustic wood chairs are cushioned in festive awning stripes. A ladder to the rooftop is a romantic gesture.

◆ Because this deck on Long Island, New York's, south shore (*left*) gets a good dose of sun and wind, owner Joseph Pricci opted for a sturdy white canvas awning. It acts as a buffer from the light and guarantees the deck's usefulness, no matter what the weather. At the rear end of the terrace, just outside glass doors, is a wood-sided whirlpool.

◆ At the height of summer's heat, just the sight of water is refreshing. At a California residence (*right*), the dining terrace commands a poolside view. An umbrella set directly into the terrace pavement provides a broad canopy to shield poolside loungers from sun. Surrounded by cooling greenery, the terrace also serves as the perfect vantage point from which to supervise young swimmers.

◆ A Spanish mission influence is evident in the architecture of this majestic old home in Tuxedo Park, New York. On the terrace (*opposite*), red geraniums, dracaena and vinca in stone garden urns accentuate the brickwork bordering the tall arched windows. A white marble table and wrought-iron chairs are used for enjoying the sweeping view of the lake or simply for overlooking the garden below.

The terrace has a host of romantic associations, and recalls the hillside gardens of Italy. Those homeowners fortunate enough to have a terrace should exploit this architectural flourish from the past to its fullest. It is really a variation on the patio, but has a dash more glamour. For romantics, the terrace conjures up images of sophisticated, Gatsby-style parties and people in full evening dress. The terrace makes a dramatic stage for evening cocktails and dancing, extravagant breakfasts and candlelit dinners, especially when enchanced by carefully chosen plantings or scented flowers so that it is redolent with fragrance on summer days and nights.

Well-sited trees on the property can shade and surround the terrace with their foliage, and potted plants situated on the walls of the terrace are classic motifs. Such containers should be made of a heavy material so that they do not topple over the side. Appoint a terrace with a collection of antique pots or Versailles-style tubs for a classical look. Container plantings can even be used to make the transition from the interior of the house to the terrace more graceful. Simply use the same style of containers in the indoor room as you do outdoors, and flank the terrace entrance with these potted plants to draw the eye effortlessly outdoors.

◆ Another window (*above, left*) is eternally guarded by a Grecian maiden.

◆ The beauty of the parterre (*above, right*) can best be viewed from the upstairs terrace. Concrete pathways extend to beds of shrubs and flowers. A birdbath provides a note of formality in the center ring, while down the far path, a secluded bench invites reflection.

CHAPTER FOUR

SWIMMING POOLS

Water in the garden instantly brings the senses into active play. It inspires even the most reserved guests to take a seat by the pool, dangle their feet in the water and perhaps even enjoy an impromptu swim. Its glittering surface becomes a natural focal point in a garden—a place to gather and entertain, a centerpiece for parties or barbecues on long summer evenings. Visually, a pool is a powerful design element in the landscape. The fact that it can also be used for swimming and carefree fun simply adds to its appeal. Even when it is not in use, it is a looking-glass to the sky, reflecting the gentle movements of clouds and rippling lightly as breezes pass over it. On the hottest of summer days, just the sight of water suggests coolness, so even without actually being immersed in its depths, it's possible to feel the pool's effects from afar.

Siting, size and shape all play fundamental roles in determining the impact of a pool in the outdoor room. Color, poolside plantings, even seating also influence its mood. For those who want to maximize a pool's drama, for example, fountains are an option as well. Running water is so appealing to the touch that most of us cannot resist the urge to kick off our shoes and splash our feet in it or simply cup our hands over its cooling flow. The soothing jets of water from a fountain provide restful background music to light reading in a hammock or lounge chair. It also easily lulls the poolside lounger to sleep with dreams of sweet-scented gardens.

People who prefer an informal landscape to one that is designed in a grand manner appreciate the natural-looking pool. Its shape and construction are meant to resemble a pond or stream more so than a pool. The choice between a traditional and natural-looking pool depends on your design sensibility and should harmonize with your life-style.

◆ A high, thick hedge of ivy and a red tile roof known as a *genoise* are the colorful background for an enticing pool in France (*previous page*). A rooftop rooster and an old stone bust on a pedestal preside.

◆ This swimming pool in southern Florida (*opposite*) is located on an ideal site. Slightly elevated, it affords a view of the facing bay and accepts cooling breezes from the swaying palm trees that surround it. Around the pool, everyone likes to stretch out, so the owners decided to use chaise longues exclusively instead of chairs. In this warm climate, shrubs grow to dramatic proportions, and there are always luscious flowers in bloom.

◆ At country enthusiast Mary Emmerling's weekend house, there's an old-fashioned backyard pool (*above*). It's new, but looks like it's always been there, thanks to its unassuming charm. The accumulation of real-life paraphernalia—an old inner tube, a watering can, rows of sturdy chaises and a picnic table—makes it clear that this is a pool that's really used, not just a pretty adornment for the yard. The pool's surround of brick laid in a basketweave pattern is Emmerling's low maintenance–high style solution to the very different requirements of tending to her active children and frequent guests.

L ike any other element in the garden, the effect of a pool, the impact it has on the garden's design and the practical value it adds to the property depend on how the pool and its surroundings are planned. For some, the pool is a place to exercise, for others an area to relax or to entertain; for still others it plays a supporting role within a flower garden. There are no hard-and-fast rules that the owner of a pool has to be an avid swimmer, constantly doing laps in the water, although there are compact lap pools for those who simply wish to exercise. For others who crave poolside lounging and floating lazily on rafts, the pool area should be luxurious and accommodating with generous seating, shaded by trees or a lattice or a pergola with a well-equipped cabana and a barbecue.

Pools are places around which to gather, to join family and friends for meals, game playing and casual conversation. For many months of the year it may be the most actively used feature of an outdoor room, so its design should enhance the property. A pool can easily become the focal point of the yard, especially when its design is in keeping with its surroundings.

Where the ground is level and there are no obstructions to viewing the pool, it can be surrounded by nothing more than a pristine deck and perhaps a brilliant expanse of green lawn. This simple arrangement brings drama to the yard, especially when the house itself is of a clean-lined design.

There is also the option of hiding the pool from view behind high hedges, where it becomes a surprise element in the garden. This arrangement is desirable in yards where the gardens take precedence over any other features and where the owners crave privacy. If located on a lower level of the property, a flight of stairs descending from a terrace or patio to the pool adds a touch of grandeur. A hillside swimming pool has an inherent drama, as if it were a stage on which to act out the pleasures of summertime living—whether entertaining friends with fine wines and gourmet fare on a table covered with elegant linen, or simply serving picnic food on a brightly checked tablecloth.

Aside from the traditional rectangle, there are a number of appealing shapes appropriate for the classic swimming pool. The rectangle is a great favorite of swimmers who want to get a good workout, and its simple geometry can be quite striking. But if a property is in an informal style, its distinct shape can produce a jarring effect. A pool with sensuous, curving sides gives personality to the yard and can very often capitalize on limited space. For such purposes, the elongated teardrop shape is a wonderful choice. Its whimsical, pleasing form gracefully slopes from shallow to deep water and offers the swimming advantages of a rectangular pool but is generally easier to fit into the yard.

◆ A pool takes on a whole different character at night. The water stills and becomes a mirror, reflecting all that surrounds it. Because this pool is situated next to a house with lots of windows and exterior lights (*right*), the effect is especially dramatic. Even the tubs of white geraniums can be seen in the darkness as chubby beacons of reflected light.

◆ The powerful geometry of this pool and its surround captures the eye, and this almost Shaker-like simplicity soothes it. A mix of straight edges and curves plays into the architecture of the house, and all work together for dramatic effect. The owners love to swim, and they wanted a weekend house, pool and multiple patios to take full advantage of the wide-open outdoors—in this case, the flat potato fields of eastern Long Island. With the help of architect Bruce Nagel, they got their wish. At one end of the pool (*left*), a curving shower with an "eye" of glass bricks hugs the shingled garage. The garage itself acts as a wall, shielding the pool area from neighboring properties. Near the sliding glass doors leading to the kitchen (*opposite, above left and right*), a capsule-shaped table is conveniently placed for lunch. The table on the rounded platform farthest from the house (*opposite, center*) provides yet another area for poolside conversation and offers an expansive view of freshly tilled farmland (*opposite, below left*). Flanked by modern lights, the glass bricks (*opposite, below right*) allow sunlight into the shower.

The commodious oval, equal in size and shape at both ends, creates a somewhat more formal effect. The kidney shape is another striking ornamental design. Its undulating form can be handily modified to suit the needs of the site and can even be redesigned as a free-form pool. For those with limited space, the L-shaped style of pool fits readily around a wing of the house, often making use of an otherwise unused corner, and affords a natural break that clearly separates diving and shallow areas. And for pure functionality, there is always the lap pool—not a particularly beautiful style, but one that allows exercise in yards where space is very limited.

The color of the pool's interior has a profound visual effect on the pool. White, light blue and pale green are all traditional choices and make the water appear clean, sparkling and inviting. Fainthearted swimmers appreciate the clearness and the ability to discern the bottom. Dark colors such as gray, deep blue and black, once dismissed as causing the pool water to appear murky, muddied or downright formidable, have come into their own in recent years, particularly as the choice for a constructed swimming pool that gives the appearance of a natural body of water, perhaps reminiscent of the fabled swimming hole. They also create a mirrorlike surface that beautifully reflects the sky and immediate surroundings, making dark colors a good choice for a more formal property where such symmetry is part of the design. Dark-painted pools also absorb more of the sun's warming rays and create a natural heating system. Color accents can be added with tiles. Placed around the water line, they will emphasize the lines of the pool and are available in colors as subdued as blue and gray, as exuberant as red and violet or in classic black-and-white combinations.

◆ Landscape architect Robert M. Fletcher redesigned a formerly ordinary California yard to create a spectacular outdoor room complete with a swimming pool and terrace (*previous page*). In this lavish setting, container plantings spill luxuriantly over the sides of the pool.

◆ Two views of a pool set into a Connecticut hillside show off its marvelous setting. The pool's design, conceived by owner Ira Howard Levy, harmonizes with the landscape. The lush green hills and deep blue water are cleverly played against the cool, muted tones of the flagstone terrace that surrounds the pool (*opposite, above*). The poolhouse, which replaced a stable, echoes the previous structure's shape (*opposite, below*).

◆ It looks as though this pool (*left and opposite*) appeared long before the house, and that's intentional. The owners wanted a place to swim that seemed to spring naturally from the earth. So a rugged outcropping of quarry rocks rings the water, and moss has been allowed to flourish between the poolside stones. Even the steps to the house appear as though they began as a simple stone path.

DESIGNING A NATURAL POOL

Properties that contain overgrown, wooded areas, mossy pathways, sunlit glades and wild flowers call for a natural-looking pool or pond. The natural pool is a hybrid of the completely untamed pond and the traditional swimming pool. These types of pools afford the owner all the luxuries of the classic pool but provide a more informal look—at home in the woodland glade, or on the edge of a wild flower meadow, never in the orderly world of structured rose gardens or close-mown tennis courts. The outdoor room need not be a completely ordered, formal space. The wild garden—which contains such natural touches as wild flowers, twig benches and wooded areas—is the perfect setting for a natural-looking pool. Such pools have irregular outlines and a nonlinear, casual quality, reminiscent of the old-fashioned swimming hole. In such cases, natural paving materials of local stone enhance an uncontrived effect. Rocks of all sizes around the edges give natural pools a romantic, idyllic air and make them inviting oases in the landscape. Boulders from the property often form the edges of a natural pool, and uneven slabs of rock can also be used to outline it while simultaneously acting as steps into the pool.

Thick poolside plantings of evergreens, giant ferns, ivy, grasses and other lush foliage also contribute to the sylvan look of this feature. Despite the rustic, unstudied look of the natural pool, it functions in the same way as its traditionally designed counterpart and has the same interior finish. The only difference lies in its informality, inviting water games and casual poolside get-togethers. Natural pools can also be combined with the surrounding elements of the formal pool, such as wooden decks and flagstone pavements.

◆ Fields of wild flowers and heady lavender, tall pine trees and distant mountains form a majestic setting for this hideaway pool in the European countryside (*left*). For extra color, pink oleanders are spotted around the pool. Sturdy foam mats and oversize pillows upholstered in comfortable cottons invite sunbathers to stretch out and enjoy the view. A white canvas umbrella shades a "farmer's lunch" of bread, cheese, fruit and wine—all local specialties. French garden chairs circle a café table.

If it is to serve as a surface for comfortable entertaining, the paving material adjoining the swimming pool must also be in keeping with its surroundings. Concrete is often used for its pristine, practical qualities, but bricks or flagstones set in mortar are also handsome and more adventurous choices that serve design needs in a variety of situations. Pools also look beautiful surrounded by redwood and teak decks.

Regardless of the material chosen, light, earthy but nonglaring colors usually work best and can be extended to an adjoining patio to facilitate the transition between different areas. Dark colors in general soak up too much heat for the comfort of bare feet on sunny days. Spaces serving a variety of functions can be defined by using different types of paving; for example, a wooden pool surround might adjoin a flagstone or brick patio equipped with a picnic table.

In all but the hottest climates, optimizing sun exposure is crucial to the enjoyment of a pool. Since pools and outdoor living areas are used most frequently in the afternoon, a southern or southwestern exposure is best and will lengthen the hours of warming sunshine they receive. This is especially appreciated at the beginning and end of summer, when temperatures are lower.

Another way to ensure maximum sun exposure during the swimming season is to eliminate shadows from buildings, trees or fences. Annoying glare can be avoided by placing the pool to the left or right of a line between it and the setting sun. Before adding this recreational feature to your yard, observe the daily pattern of the sun moving across it. Orient the deep end of the pool so that swimmers jump off the diving board with their backs to the sun, rather than facing it.

◆ Moving water never fails to enchant and give a feeling of refreshment, the owners of this Houston pool reasoned, so they decided to install fountains. Four streams form dramatic sparkling arches above the water (*above*). The effect is twofold: Swimmers can frolic in the overhead mist, and diners at the lavender cloth-covered table (*opposite*) can enjoy a cooling view. The terrace is made up of inlaid stones. Across the way, a latticework shelter, weathered to a warm gray and bracketed with wisteria, provides shade.

◆ Some of the elements of a Swiss chalet are at work in the architecture of this thoroughly modern poolhouse, located in Washington, D.C., and designed by J. Carlos Osorio (*opposite*). The structure—which has an A-frame roofline, timbered sides and an open glass wall—provides a stunning backdrop for the swimming pool. Large terra-cotta pots of daisies lined up in front of the house echo the sweeping curves of the pool. The glass walls enclose a sunroom, furnished by interior designer Keith Babcock (*above, left*), where French doors are usually propped open to erase any barriers between inside and out. The effect is heightened by the mauve stone floor, which continues inside from the patio, and the natural textures of wicker and wood furniture with sunset-shaded cushions. A fan stirs a lazy breeze overhead, ruffling the full petals of peonies (*above, right*) cut from the flower beds outside.

With so much sun warming the pool area, shade is particularly welcome. Having a sheltered area near the water for lounging, cooking and entertaining makes it possible to enjoy the pool all day long. Umbrellas, canvas awnings, cabanas and pergolas offer shelter from the sun while also adding diversity and splashes of color to the landscape. Overstuffed waterproof pillows as well as lightweight furniture increase the livability of the poolside area. They can be moved easily from sun to shade, so it's possible to take a morning dip and then spend the afternoon lounging in the cool shade, sipping iced tea and reading. Parents of small children should especially consider this arrangement, as it makes it possible to watch them play in the pool from a comfortable vantage point.

For those who have the space, adding a poolhouse or cabana is a wise idea. A poolhouse equipped with dressing room, bathroom, shower and even a cushion-filled corner in which to relax after an invigorating swim is one of life's greatest luxuries. Such structures are also supremely practical, keeping dripping-wet swimmers from entering the house.

◆ This pool gets its graphic
punch from an edging of
crisp black-and-white tiles
and the sharp shadows of
an open-air breezeway cast
against the deck and
poolhouse wall (*right*). Fitting neatly into this tropical
environment, a quartet of
classic Adirondack chairs
and twin benches are often
arranged in the shade as the
setting for a poolside lunch.
If the sun has had a chance
to warm the deck, it's the
perfect place to stretch out
after a swim (*above*). Sher-
bet-colored striped pillows
and towels stand out vividly
in the intense sun.

Plantings are the finishing touches of poolside areas and play a principal role in how the pool relates to its surroundings. Some people opt for a classic hedge to frame the pool. Evergreen hedges offer the advantage of not dropping their leaves into the pool. Immaculately clipped hedges of box or yew suggest a level of formality that harmonizes with statuary and urns.

Containers are natural choices for pool areas, serving to brighten and soften the stone or brick of a patio. Sizable wood tubs and large terra-cotta pots are attractive choices. For maximum drama and color impact, mass the containers in corners of the pool surround. The most satisfactory plants for poolside plantings are those that please you, in colors that complement the surrounding architectural materials and furnishings. If the pool area is used in the evening or later at night, all-white and nocturnally scented flowers are delightful natural amenities, especially such plants as Queen Anne's lace, white summer phlox, baby's breath, white flowering tobacco, scented-leaf geraniums and lemon verbena. White bedding geraniums, white periwinkles, white petunias and white everblooming begonias are also excellent, as well as tree-form standard roses, particularly in a free-blooming, sweet-smelling cultivar such as 'Class Act,' an award-winning floribunda. Don't plant any of these too close to the pool, as they may attract insects and bees to the poolside.

◆ Tropical turtles, both real and imaginary, populate the waters of these natural-looking pools in the house of architect Edward Giddings in Cabo San Lucas, Mexico. On a covered patio (*opposite*), high-backed chairs gather around a glass-topped table. The table base is a carved stone monkey, in keeping with the south-of-the-border location. Beside the pool, a genuine turtle rests on the rocky edge, about to test the waters. Striped canvas pillows invite visitors to recline and run their fingers through the water. In the balcony pool, marking the border between swimming pool and whirlpool, a clay turtle (*above*) crawls beneath the shadows of a sheltering palm on the pool's blue mosaic edge.

CHAPTER FIVE

LITTLE RETREATS

We all feel the need to get away from it all at some time or another. Ideally, this should be possible without spending stressful time traveling. Everyone is entitled to a little retreat at home, a magical space for relaxation only a few short steps from the door. This chapter explores a variety of imaginative exits from the fast lane into secret gardens and rooms where we can escape the pressures of everyday life.

The single most important thing to remember about a little retreat is its primary purpose: a place to relax and unwind. In order for workaday cares to vanish into thin air, simplicity must be the golden rule. If the little retreat becomes too fraught with details of maintenance and upkeep, then you may find yourself returning to work before long. Implicit in this is that the retreat must indeed be "little," in the sense that it won't be overly large, complicated or demanding. The accessibility of a retreat is also essential to its success. Part of the little retreat's allure is that you are not there daily, that it is such a break from the everyday. But if the retreat is too remote or too distant, then it will be used far less than it should. In spirit and style, rather than location, a retreat should be removed from daily routine.

The key ingredients to this are a playfulness and a relaxed, easygoing style. If this is a place to let go of our self-involvement, so too can it be a place to let go with furnishings and accessories: a place to display found objects from long walks and sentimental keepsakes and a home for pieces of old furniture. A converted barn or garden shed, a lattice-walled gazebo, a cozy summer cottage, even a secluded garden seat can serve as a personal retreat. These are places for relaxation and spiritual restoration—nothing too large, nothing too self-conscious or rule-bound, and nothing too complicated or dependent on gadgetry is allowed.

◆ A quintessential woodland gazebo (*previous page*) built into a hillside is a fairy-tale setting. The shady garden was designed to entertain its owners with a constant parade of color throughout warm months. In spring, the French parterre beds include peonies and irises, shasta daisies, spiky lavender agapanthus and deep-purple salvia and are edged with fluffy gray lamb's ears and broadleafed hostas. Within the wisteria-draped gazebo, white lace and wicker look cool and fresh.

◆ One of man's earliest retreats, the unpretentious hammock is utterly idyllic. The sweeping limbs of this willow (*opposite*) are sufficient support for an old rope hammock.

◆ The perennial border (*above*) is a soft backdrop for an antique garden bench at Pam Kay's home in Maine. Its craggy good looks come from years of sitting out in all kinds of weather. In a garden designed by Nancy McCabe, foxgloves enjoy a long blooming season and provide rich pink color that plays off the dewy grass.

The simplest of all retreats are the private corners of a garden kept comfortable and secluded by tall plantings. Here, quiet hours can be spent on a bench or in a hammock. Seclusion is an important part of a little retreat, and garden seating can be positioned behind tall shrubs or waving grasses or in a natural glade obscured from view, or visible only from afar. Other charming locations for little retreats are nearby flower borders, where the garden visitor can breathe in sweet floral fragrances and observe the constant activity of bees and birds. These kinds of spaces are as much for wiling away long summer afternoons as for lazing with a good book on blustery fall days. In a sense, they are the purest form of the little retreat, because they principally rely on nature for their design and require minimal adjustments to be made into private spaces.

The most straightforward furniture option and the most enticing in its invitation to relax is the hammock. Gently swinging back and forth beneath a dappled, leafy canopy is one of the simplest and most soothing of outdoor pleasures. Hanging the hammock from the limbs of a stately tree ensures that it will be shaded throughout the summer.

Traditional garden seats and benches also enhance outdoor living. They usually do not have pads, cushions or other upholstery. In a very real sense their freedom from maintenance is a trade-off for hardness and a certain lack of creature comfort. The idea is for a refreshing pause, not settling in for a long rest. Despite all this, it is possible to find garden furniture that is as pleasing to the body as to the eye. If your property has an outstanding view, be sure to locate these seats to take advantage of the panorama. Having a view imparts a sense of dominion and is an important device in landscape design because it expands the scope of your property beyond mere physical boundaries.

The bench is a basic yet vital piece of garden furniture. Metal garden benches, from antique to new, are usually cast in some garden motif, such as ferns, grapevines or wild flowers. They are equally at home in both formal and wild gardens. Such benches harmonize especially well with Victorian-theme gardens, which often incorporate lacy metal fences and gates as well as jardinieres and other exuberant touches. Antique stone benches and contemporary ones of cast concrete are among the most popular choices in all kinds of gardens. The stone bench is a classic, enduring style that stands up to all kinds of weather and doesn't require maintenance. It is best to give some forethought to locating such a bench in the garden, because it is not readily moved about to suit whims.

◆ Pulled to this spot last year, a couple of Adirondack chairs (*left*) haven't been moved since. Facing a pair of antique stone gateposts and, beyond, the ocean at the edge of the property, the chairs seem at peace with the world.

◆ This isn't Japan, it's Houston, Texas, but the lines of the latticework shelter (*above*) and pillow-covered garden bench have an Oriental air. A mood of quiet serenity pervades this hideaway, and stopping here for a moment is irresistible. Underfoot, the pebbled concrete floor is edged with a double row of bricks. The greenery is distinctly southern; crape myrtle, photinia and plumeria all flourish in the filtered light.

There are as many choices of style, finish and color for garden seats and benches as there are for sofas and couches employed indoors. They may be old or new, rustic or sophisticated, with or without backs and arms. The most basic piece of furniture comes from the garden itself: a large split log, flat side up, mounted on two log posts anchored in the ground and rising above to a comfortable level for seating.

Wood is a popular choice for outdoor furniture because it blends so effortlessly with the color and texture of trees in the yard. It also weathers beautifully. Choices include the plain teak bench often associated with English country gardens, the rolled-arm and curved-back bench designed by Sir Edwin Lutyens, and a variety of Chippendale-influenced fretwork designs. Rustic twig-constructed chairs, tables and benches actually enhance their natural surroundings. Similarly, the classic Adirondack-style furniture, painted white, off-white, or gray-blue complements any outdoor room.

◆ Having a little retreat doesn't always mean getting away from it all. In West Virginia, a wild-flower fence stakes out the border of this seating area right in the middle of the pasture (*opposite, above and below*). Perhaps it's the Victorian lace doily on the table that makes this seem a proper outpost for enjoying lemonade. A pair of twig chairs and a bushel basket of tall, white-flowering weeds look so natural here, it is as if they were themselves fashioned from the surrounding woods.

◆ The mother of two young boys, garden designer Nancy McCabe created private space for her sons by converting an old shed (*above*) into a playhouse. Set into a slope at the back of her garden, the tiny building can be a lookout for pirates and other invaders; a nearby boulder might be a ship's prow. Inside (*right*), furnishings are simple and, importantly, hard-wearing: an old trunk under a faded hooked rug, Lloyd loom wicker chairs, floor cushions covered in a fern print and fishing gear at the ready. Egg-yolk-yellow balls in several sizes are involved in an endless variety of games.

◆ Designer Ron Grimaldi found this rare wood and zinc gazebo (*left*) on a trip to England, and immediately made arrangements to have it installed in his garden at Rose Hall in New York. Navy-and-white draperies hug the stanchions on balmy days and are drawn when the weather turns.

◆ In Seaside, Florida, a shelter in the sand (*opposite, above*) brings to mind a Gothic solarium. In this planned community, the gazebo serves as a gathering spot for local homeowners, who have established a weekly tradition of serving late afternoon tea beneath it.

◆ A classic white latticework gazebo with pointed roof (*opposite, below*) and a white picket fence are companionably paired in a recently designed Long Island, New York, garden. When the gazebo was built, the owner surrounded it with an exuberant mix of annuals and perennials. Constructed soon after the property was acquired, the gazebo was the only source of shade while the trees were still young saplings.

Beyond the elementary hideaway that includes nothing more than a place to sit in leafy surroundings is the structural retreat, which can be called a pagoda, summerhouse, arbor or gazebo. The more enclosed this type of garden retreat, the greater its usefulness in rainy or chilly weather. A surrounding of deciduous trees serves to shade and cool the space in summer while allowing more warming sunlight to penetrate in spring and fall. Adding fabric-covered roll-up screens or curtains also provides temporary enclosure and protection from wind and rain.

Gazebos and similar rustic domains may be placed to advantage even in the smallest of gardens. Located within a few steps of the house, the gazebo is a convenient spot for meals at any time of day. To create a sense of division between a gazebo and the yard on a small property, simple elevate it a step or two higher than the surrounding surface, which may be paved or cultivated. This heightens the sense of walking into another world, of stepping up to enter a special, private place.

A gazebo or any open-air summerhouse can also be accommodated in the most distant reaches of a property. Where there is a sharp change in grade, the gazebo can be located to take advantage of a view. If the idea of retreating from civilization entirely is appealing, locate the structure where there is no view of the house. This reinforces the sense of being far away. A meandering path leading up to a gazebo with plants spilling out over its edges creates a further division between the everyday world of the home and the romantic, somewhat mysterious realm of the garden gazebo.

Because they so resemble interior rooms, gazebos and similar structures lend themselves naturally to furnishings. However, you shouldn't view furnishing your garden retreat as a full-scale decorating job. Instead, consider the practicalities and add minimal embellishment. Any furniture brought in should stand up to all types of weather or at least be lightweight and portable. A simple solution is to only add built-in seating. This is particularly wonderful because it can be used year-round, to enjoy the lovely weather in spring, summer and autumn and to take in breathtaking snowy views in winter. For more formal occasions, add a table and chairs for dining, for playing games such as bridge or backgammon or for enjoying a summer tea party.

◆ On a rambling property in southern California, a pergola with vine-covered eaves (*opposite and above*) offers diners sun-dappled seclusion. The table in this tunnel of greenery is set for a leisurely meal with a centerpiece of primroses fresh from the nursery. The pergola resembles a Grecian ruin. This effect is enhanced by its columns and skeletal arching roof, which is overgrown by a tumble of bougainvillea, roses and geraniums. It serves as an ideal vantage point for viewing tennis matches on the red clay courts below.

PLANNING AN OFFICE RETREAT

Some of us define work as pleasure and derive a sense of satisfaction from it. Locating an office in a private retreat allows for greater concentration on work while also providing a serene feeling of privacy so often lacking in a bustling household. In order to successfully convert a retreat into an office, you must first assess what can be left intact and what needs to be altered. Beautiful features of old buildings such as rough-hewn beams in barns and exposed brick in old outbuildings should be retained and even played up visually. Try to find new applications for existing structural quirks. For example, a silo could be converted into a multi-story retreat. Or add a conventional door to a garage or barn and use the old oversize doors as movable walls.

If the office is going to be used as a crafts workshop, shelves and proper tool storage are essential. Whether you design jewelry, create floral arrangements or work with textiles, your work involves a number tools that create too much clutter if they don't get put away properly. To create as streamlined an effect as possible, shelves can easily be hidden behind doors that slide shut or open like cupboards. A trolley for mobile storage is also useful and can act as a catchall for loose items. If there are no closets, decorative freestanding cabinets can hold an assortment of items while bringing visual interest to the office retreat.

Writers require storage for books as well as a sturdy table that is big enough to accommodate a typewriter or a computer and printer. A dramatic full wall of shelves is a good solution, as it conserves space yet is also attractive. The shelves need not be completely filled with books, however; a display area can hold collectibles. Artists especially need light. This may mean that you will have to add windows, enlarge existing windows, exchange a solid door for sliding glass doors or even add skylights.

In a retreat and guest-house in upstate New York designed by Trumbull Associates, a dramatic wall of windowpanes overlooks the great outdoors. But the resident here turns her back, and nothing distracts from the work at hand in this pristine office (*opposite*). The clutter—the inevitable by-product of paperwork—is neatly stored in two free-standing cupboards. The scrubbed pine floor looks its honeyed best surrounded by all this whiteness. On the desk, a bunch of cosmos offers a double dose of color.

No heat, no lights are necessary in this room when the sunshine does its duty (*right, above*). Candlestick lamps with marbled shades cast their light on the subject after hours. The typing table on casters can be rolled about at will or stored when it's not being used. If a refreshing walk outdoors is called for, it's just a step away. The hexagonal entryway to the office (*right, below*) leads to a hall, where a row of shelves house favorite books and the owner's collection of carved shore birds. Beyond the office is a small kitchen and upstairs a handy bedroom for guests.

◆ Outside the barn-inspired retreat (*left and above*), the symmetry and graphic features of the structure contrast strikingly with the placid landscape. The house shape and windowpane motif are repeated in its various components. The office is clearly visible from the slate patio outdoors, where two tables and chairs are all it takes to make a lovely setting. A great supply of seasoned wood is stacked in its own little angular "barn."

◆ A tiny crystal palace by the water's edge (*opposite, above*) cradles a bubbling whirlpool within. This graceful glass outpost had been neglected for years when it was inherited and restored by New York interior designer Susan Zises Green. By day, the glass house sparkles in the sunshine (*opposite, below left*). At night, the moon and stars and some indirect lighting form a simple canopy. Coordinating chintzes cushion the wicker chairs and love seat. The newly installed whirlpool (*opposite, below right*) is elevated and hugs one side of the room.

◆ A long view of the glass house (*above*) shows how it was built into the hillside. This careful placement meant the family would be embraced by a view of lawns and woodlands.

Another type of outbuilding that is easily converted into a little retreat is the greenhouse. Since running water and electricity are usually already installed in an existing greenhouse, it can be converted to human comforts fairly easily. While such a unit may have been planned originally to serve only the needs of a dedicated gardener and the plants, a new owner may wish to minimize this and make the greenhouse an inviting, oasislike retreat where even cold or rainy weather can be enjoyed from warmth and comfort.

There are a number of beautiful glass garden structures that don't necessarily have to be used for growing plants. These are designed in a variety of shapes and make ideal shelters for hot tubs, as they allow natural light to stream in or stars to shine overhead while protecting the bather from the whims of the weather. They also can be furnished as minimally or elaborately as other little retreats, as well as with lush greenery of all kinds. Decorating and furnishing a little retreat that affords shelter from the elements is for many of us one of life's unique pleasures. Common sense dictates easy care and as little upkeep as possible. Simple, functional window treatments as well as basic, durable furniture are all that is needed to make the retreat comfortable.

Somewhere between the definition of the open-air gazebo and the weekend home lies the enclosed little retreat. This term describes a small house composed of one or more enclosed rooms. The difference between the enclosed retreat and the home is much greater than that of size, however. The retreat is meant for light-hearted, pleasurable pursuits only. While such a building may stand close by or may even be attached to the main dwelling, it usually stands at some distance from the house proper. How far you can go with such amenities as electricity, plumbing, heating and cooling is determined by the way you plan to use the space.

How you use an enclosed retreat depends on its size and your interests. A place for reading or general relaxation needn't be very large and might be outfitted as simply as placing a futon or narrow mattress on the floor with lots of comfy pillows. An enclosed little retreat may be occupied for an hour or a day, a weekend, a fortnight or for an extended period of time in which the temperatures are mostly in a range for human comfort. If the retreat is used often and becomes a place to prepare meals or relax after a swim in a nearby lake, it must be equipped with such basic amenities as running water, a kitchen, a bath and electricity. Whether or not you allow a telephone into the inner sanctum of retreat is a most personal option; each such convenience you bring to your hideaway tends to make it more like what you are escaping from. Yet some of us may not feel at ease without this communication with the outside world.

It's a good idea to situate a little retreat so that it is conducive to outdoor activities. A flat, level area cleared of rocks near the retreat is a wonderful place to hang a volleyball net or set up a croquet game. If you're lucky enough to have a body of water on your property, by all means situate your retreat by the side of a lake, stream or pond. This opens up possibilities for swimming, fishing and boating. Old boathouses are ideal candidates for refurbishment as retreats. They usually are connected to a dock or pier of some kind, which is a natural choice for use as a patio for easy entertaining. Add a few umbrellas, and the boathouse dock becomes a perfectly agreeable place to spend an afternoon.

◆ Down a steeply sloping path at the bottom of a wooded hillside (*opposite*), this boathouse sits in calm seclusion by the shores of New York's Tuxedo Lake. Those who relish water and the sound of lapping waves always find the calm they're looking for here. The floating docks are perfect places for soaking up the sun.

◆ Another boathouse in Tuxedo Park nestles into its plot (*above*), its port side dotted with porthole windows that project a nautical theme. The mansard roof has a charming flair with practical roots: It sheds the rain with abandon. A rock wall frames the boathouse on both sides and shores up the land beyond.

◆ At designer John Saladino's boathouse—on his weekend retreat in Connecticut—the living is as rustic as the surroundings: The structure has no electricity, plumbing or heat. In the rough-timbered great room (*left*), the mass of wild flowers that fills the stone fireplace in summer will be replaced by crackling logs at the first sign of frost. By setting the food out in one central spot, everyone can help themselves whenever they wish. The buffet table gets its frothy fringe from a ring of cress.

◆ The design of the boathouse creates graceful transitions from indoors to outdoors. Deep casement windows (*opposite, above left*) are left open on warm days for an uninterrupted view of the pond. The shuttered kitchen window (*opposite, above right*) serves as a pass-through both before and after mealtime. Twin topiaries flank the window, standing sentry during the meal. More informal meals are also taken on the dock (*opposite, below*), which is conveniently located just outside the house.

Cabins of all kinds make wonderful retreats, and in their down-to-earth simplicity they afford an immediate sense of being close to nature. A porch or stoop looking out onto plantings or wilderness is a restful place to sit. Inside the cabin retreat, a fireplace can provide warmth. It's also useful to have a fully equipped kitchen, but an outdoor campfire or grill can easily suffice and make the experience of visiting the retreat seem more like a nature trek. If there's no running water, a stream or pond nearby can return bathing to its origins.

Creative types in search of silence in which to discern the spirits of the muses truly appreciate a cabin, which can feel more remote than it is in actuality. However, since we are by nature social creatures, little retreats aren't necessarily for one or two people alone. When a cabin isn't being used for contemplative reasons, it should be opened up to accommodate a crowd for a picnic. With cold in the air and snow all around, even a tiny cottage in a woodland clearing or at the edge of a field can afford a warm retreat for skiers and other outdoors types in need of a hot drink and friendly company. A roaring campfire is particularly delightful for an outdoor party in autumn or winter, and guests will never become uncomfortable because they can simply slip indoors when they feel a chill coming on.

◆ Outdoor living needn't stop at the end of summer. Frosty weather is just the point of this picnic in the snow. It's the reward to look forward to after an afternoon of cross-country skiing. The roaring bonfire (*above*) is enough to warm even the chilliest fingers and toes. It also sheds light on the portable feast laid out on a tartan blanket. The fixings include steaming mugs of hot mulled cider and a basket of savory meat pies that are easy to eat by hand—a mittened hand! Fat wedges of cheese are simple to transport, and they hold up in the icy air. The rustic boathouse (*opposite, above*) has a second life as a way station for winter sports and recreations such as these. Over the years, it has

hosted all manner of celebrations, from the humblest (coffee and sandwiches) to the most celebratory (Champagne and hors d'oeuvres). Here, on a weathered trestle table, a Navajo blanket is the colorful backdrop for a buffet of grilled lemon-ginger chicken, potato salad and crusty breads. At the boathouse (*opposite, below left*), returning skiers prepare for refreshment, while frolicking children get their refreshment from building forts and throwing snowballs. Returning home (*opposite, below right*), skiers find dessert served a stone's throw from the house.

◆ County animals enjoy the tranquility of little retreats as much as people do. A custom-designed circular birdhouse sits high above the energy of the garden (*left*).

◆ For other birds, prime real estate can be found in a surprising variety of places (*opposite*). A knotty branch (*above, left*) raises a basic birdhouse to new heights. What's good for the goose is a stucco toolshed with a folksy twig fence (*above, right*). A bird barn boasts few amenities but still draws an entourage of squatters to perch inside its walls (*below, left*). A birdhouse with a view and a fireplace (*below, right*) attracts a better class of bird.

CHAPTER SIX

GARDENS

Good planning is the basis of any successful garden design. In setting out to create a garden, we must make decisions about the style we seek and whether the garden should serve ornamental or practical purposes or both. The garden type you choose should be compatible with the amount of energy and time you are willing to give to it.

Formal gardens requiring constant upkeep are not a realistic option for families with limited time for outdoor maintenance. Far more practical would be a garden of minimum-care flowering shrubs and trees left to grow naturally. On the other hand, it's possible to establish gardens that seem elaborate but are actually easy to create. Beds of brightly blooming annuals, planted in succession so that they flower from spring until autumn, create a lavish look in the garden that doesn't require a great deal of time to plant or maintain. Above all, gardening should never become a chore. Gardening is a hobby, a productive form of relaxation from which we derive immeasurable pleasure. It keeps us attuned to the seasonal cycles of nature while also bringing us tangible rewards, not only in its beauty, but in its harvest of vegetables, herbs and flowers.

In designing your garden, you have the same range of options as does the interior designer. Combining plant materials involves working with color, form and texture and arranging them in a pleasing composition. As with the interior of your home, the garden should have a distinct style and not look pieced together. On a small lot, it is especially important that the garden is well planned. Although you may desire to have a rich variety of plants on your property, an average-size yard will begin to look like a horticultural hodgepodge if you do not streamline your plantings. The key to giving your garden personality and visual appeal lies in creating a space that brings pleasure year-round.

◆ Pansies show their sweet faces to all who enter this enchanting circular garden (*previous page*). Stones were set into the lawn in a starburst pattern to delineate the shape of the plantings and put the focus on the big ceramic urn that anchors the center circle. The wrought-iron garden bench is framed by a crude shelter of wooden poles that might have been lashed together in moonlight by some diligent forest elves. Peonies, iris, and a young laurel tree are right at home in this plot of semishade.

◆ The traditional American village plot is revived at this home in Kinderhook, New York (*opposite*). In a garden so timeless it could have looked just like this a hundred years ago, a romantic afternoon tea will drift on into early evening. When it is viewed from the antique wicker of the back porch, the garden is framed by delicate fretwork. In another, more formal garden (*above*), a band of moss-covered elephants have selected an old stone bench for taking their sunbath. Unlike those created of shrubs and hedges, these topiary pachyderms are quite portable and enjoy traveling about their garden in the Delaware Valley.

Specialty gardens, devoted entirely to one type of flower, are highly rewarding and appeal to gardeners with a passion for collecting. The most popular flower for such gardens is the rose, but there are also intriguing possibilities for collecting violets and pansies, daffodils, lilies and peonies. The specialty garden does not have to flower all in a burst. By planting a variety of species that flower at different times of year, it's possible to prolong the blooming period.

Another way of indulging a taste for the unusual is the topiary garden. Topiary involves shearing upright-growing plants, such as rosemary, box and yew, into a variety of figures and shapes. This ancient garden art is a traditional element in formal gardens, where it takes on elaborate sculptural forms. But topiary can also have an element of playfulness about it. When plants are sculpted into animal forms, they become wonderful, fanciful touches for a formal garden.

A love of gardens often begins at an early age, with a fascination for flower and scent and green leaves. Children have a natural affinity for growing things and enjoy the process of digging, sowing seeds, watering and waiting. They are thrilled by the appearance of a few early, plucky leaves and will lavish care on even a tiny patch of soil. Cordon off a sunny section of garden, and help your child plant hearty vegetables and annuals.

◆ On this New England property, house and garden seem to reach out and embrace each other naturally. Each captures the unassuming, imaginative spirit of the other so that the entire property blends seamlessly. Hand-carved railings incorporating a whimsical heart-shaped finial overlook a pergola, which runs from the house above the courtyard garden (*opposite*).

◆ Over three hundred perennials are massed in this entrance garden, in a rich tapestry of textures and colors that spills over paths and porch alike (*above*). From the lawn, the easy blend of house and garden is most visible (*below*). Although the house is new, it has been built in a traditional "farmhouse" style, with individualistic details that reflect the owners' abiding involvement with folk-art-inspired handicrafts. Garden fence and gate are designed in a rustic style, while the homemade storage shed is enlivened by hand-carved detailing in its windows.

◆ Every garden is a reflection of its creator, and like fingerprints, no two gardens can ever be identical. Even with the same basic elements—flowers and shrubs, fences and footpaths—each garden will be unique. In an English-style garden created by Doris Magowan and the landscape designer Robert Welsh (*left, above*), the white-picket fence, latticework gazebo and irrepressible cottage flowers are immediately appealing. The English Cotswolds inspired the fence in Isabel and Winston Fowlkes' lush garden (*left, below*). When it was inherited, the garden had dozens of peonies; the couple filled out the herbaceous borders to achieve a "beauty that is appropriate and disciplined." The Crowninshield garden (*opposite, above*) is a romantic ruin on an 1800s powder mill in the Delaware Valley. The garden was the passion of its owners, who transformed the industrial site into terraced gardens that pay homage to those of the Italian Renaissance. In contrast to the Crowninshield garden, which has soothing green tones, this wildflower garden in Tuxedo Park, New York (*opposite, below*), dazzles the eye with vibrant color, with its mix of pink and white daises and marigolds.

The cutting garden is another option for the outdoor room. This garden can be as decorative as it is attractive. If well planned, even a small cutting garden can provide an abundance of flowers to decorate your home. Remember to plant flowers in colors that harmonize with your interior design. White flowers are especially good choices because they can be matched with any interior decor. Pastel-colored and miniature flowers are at home in a romantic, antique-filled room. Bright-hued and distinctively shaped flowers are such strong design elements that they tend to look best displayed against a plain backdrop.

Plant a mixture of bulbs, annuals and perennials so that you can enjoy flowers from spring until autumn. You can collect daffodils and tulips from the cutting garden in spring. In the summertime, roses, calendulas, irises, snapdragons and violets, among many other species, can be harvested from the cutting garden. And in autumn, nasturtiums and chrysanthemums create vividly colored bouquets. If a cutting garden is large and informally planted, it can be sited within full view of the home, as bare spaces left when flowers are harvested won't be so noticeable. A small cutting garden planted in rows can even be incorporated with the vegetable patch.

◆ The best cutting gardens (*above*) offer shoulder-to-shoulder blossoms in a variety of colors, in a continuously evolving selection. When flowers are this abundant, they can be arranged in an endless variety of bouquets for the house, from an extravagant dining table centerpiece to incidental nosegays and tussie-mussies that are tucked into unexpected corners.

◆ Morning is the best time to harvest flowers, while the dew is still on them. Plunging the stems into a bucket of cool water (*opposite*) is a good method of keeping them looking fresh. These newly clipped posies will soon be arranged into free-form bouquets for decorations throughout the house, as well as for outdoors on the family's porch.

Some of the most im-
pressive gardens are not
grand but casual in their
design. A garden in Tuxedo
Park, New York (*above*), is
so thick with flowers that it
resembles a wild-flower
meadow, yet it lends drama
to the yard just as effectively
as a formal garden would.
In Ryan Gainey's southern
garden (*right*), cottage-style
beds bloom in glorious informality. An ornamental
urn acts as a traditional
focal point in this otherwise
unconventional garden.

◆ On sunny days, the fragrance of this herb garden is particularly seductive. Pungent scents—is it rosemary? is it bay?—come wafting along on the breeze. Its appeal also derives from the charming objects that furnish the space. An old bookcase (*this page, above*) still holds volumes—volumes of herbs and flowers. Four rosemary standards fly like flags in the background, a silver helichrysum plant flourishes on the bench, while animal figurines keep watch from a shadier perch down below. The view from the garden toward the house (*this page, below, left*) shows the design of the land, with plants laid out in mixed beds separated by red-brick walkways. A potting bench is set up by the house, so it's easy to give plants with pinched toes a new footing. Tidy patches of herbs and flowers (*this page, below, right*) are meticulously bedded in front of a spruce-green trellised "doorway" that beckons to parts unknown. The trellis is framed by a clipped hemlock hedge. Near the old potting shed (*opposite*), a stately twig chair takes the form of an old man resting, hands on knees. He surveys the scene of neatly laid beds from his perch at the end of an aged stone path. Large shrubs have been allowed to prosper as a backdrop for the assortment of low-growing bushy herbs.

◆ A bird's-eye view of this vegetable garden (*opposite*) near the New Jersey shore gives an idea of its scope and grandeur. The garden has always occupied this sunny, slightly sloping piece of land, for everything thrives here! The two-wheeled cart will soon overflow with an abundance of well-tended veggies that are harvested daily. Lettuces started indoors are usually the first to be savored; some of the beans are still being picked as frost approaches from the north. This straw basket (*right, above*) is just the right size for a supper's worth of salad fixings. The peppers will be roasted on the grill. The main ingredients for the aforementioned salad are baby oak-leaf lettuce and tomatoes (*right, below*).

If you're enthralled by the elusive fragrance of freesia or particularly enjoy the aroma of creeping thyme that is released when you walk across it, then you may wish to create a garden of pleasingly scented plants. Some plants release their fragrance especially at nighttime. Among them are night-scented stock, sweet rocket, flowering tobacco, mock orange and Madonna lily.

Herbs in general are wonderful choices for the scented garden. These versatile plants also serve numerous other purposes. Lavender and lemon balm are among the most fragrant of herbs. Bee-balm, the scented-leaf geraniums, sweet cicely, lavender-cotton, the sweet old-fashioned nasturtiums, violets, lemon verbena, sweet woodruff and tansy are also scented herbs.

If you want your herb garden to serve multiple purposes, plant a number of culinary herbs as well. These form the core of any herb garden and also have pleasant scents. Chives, parsley, dill, basil, rosemary, thyme, mint, chervil and tarragon are the chief cooking herbs. If you have enough space and want to stock your pantry with more unusual herbs, also plant marjoram, sage, anise, caraway, savory, angelica and horseradish.

Herb plots usually look most striking when they are laid out in neat, orderly rows. A pretty effect can be created in a small space by planting herbs in radiating rows surrounding a focal point, such as a birdbath, astrolabe or sculpture.

◆ In southern France (*above*), rows of fragrant, bushy lavender line the sides of a grassy trail. The lavender plantings stop just short of a tall hedgerow that delineates one end of this scented field.

◆ In a corner of a garden-side drying shed (*opposite*), an old table is a hive of activity. When it's time to sort and arrange the scented garden's bounty of dill seed, rosemary, tansy, lemon verbena, sage, lavender flowers, roses and costmary, no other place will do. (A drying shed could just as easily be a portion of an airy garage or attic.) Some of the flowers are bound with string and hung upside-down to dry at once. Other cuttings are temporarily set in baskets and will be fashioned into herbal wreaths, bouquets and scented potpourris. Seed packets tossed in a wooden bowl have been carefully marked with the date the seeds were planted and when they bloomed. All this information will be recorded in a gardening journal at the end of the season, when the outdoor chores of summer have waned.

◆ A house in town didn't deter London florist Kenneth Turner from enjoying the out-of-doors. He made the most of the small patio out back, and decorated the indoors like a garden. In the dining room (*opposite, above*), the table is always set with a floral floor-length cloth, and the centerpiece is a starlit landscape of candles and potted blossoms. Even the chairs are dressed in flowery sheaths. Outside, a new fence was called for, along with climbing vines and lots of potted plants.

Framing the back lot with a tall, thin-slatted fence complements the architecture of the house (notice the high, thin Gothic windows in the dining room). The bust of a Grecian maiden sits in repose amid pots of Easter roses, tree-form Boston daisies, pink hydrangea, and green dwarf boxwood (*above and opposite, above*). Some other spectacular results have been achieved with Boston daisy and pale pink hydrangea grown in pots (*opposite, below left*). The outdoor table and chairs (*opposite, below right*) serve alternately as a potting table and a place to enjoy dinners alfresco.

Designing an urban garden presents a variety of challenges. To become transformed into a livable space, a pocket-size yard must provide privacy and also have a pleasing design. To satisfy the first requirement, you may wish to erect walls or fences if none exist. Flower beds can be planted in front of these, and vines can be trained along them to soften the effect.

Grass is not a good choice for the ground cover of a city garden because it can be difficult to grow in urban conditions and needs upkeep. Paving is a more practical option for underfoot surfaces, and also allows you to create different gradations within the site. A change of level tends to make a garden look larger than it actually is and also de-emphasizes narrowness.

The town garden is often sited at a disadvantage, since nearby buildings block sunlight and make gardening more of a challenge. To keep your town garden thriving, select plants that grow well in shade. A shrub border might contain juneberry, dogwood, winterberry and viburnum. Vines such as Dutchman's pipe, honeysuckle and fox grape tolerate shade and can be used to create a leafy, private bower in an urban backyard.

◆ Some say a garden just outside the door is the easiest to take care of and enjoy: These two gardens prove the point. The stucco house (*opposite*) is graced with a tiny patio off the dining room. The pair of resident golden Labs like to sun themselves on the warm flagstones. Because the owners like flowers but don't want to fuss over them, all the plantings are purposely low-maintenance. The scattered plantings of lady's mantle, purple sweet rocket, yellow potentilla and shrub roses as well as the grassy sedges, lily turf and euphorbia by the steps are all quite content to thrive on benign neglect. The chair by the door has a regular occupant; most days, the owner reads his afternoon paper here. What used to be a neglected back entranceway (*right*) was transformed into an inviting flower garden. Lythrum 'Morden Pink,' tall flowering tobacco and cosmos bring color to the tiny plot. Brick paths are a civilizing note, leading to the graceful garden bench.

PLANTING A YEAR-ROUND GARDEN

When winter comes to the garden, the landscape can often end up looking depressingly bare. Although a few colorful berries and the seedheads and pods of some flowers may remain on the plants, most gardens lose their vibrancy in winter. An easy way to counteract the winter doldrums is to plant an evergreen garden. Both needle- and broad-leaved species should be incorporated in the design, with a range of hues from light green to blue to red. Japanese and English holly are lovely choices and impart mass and depth to the garden with their crisp green foliage. Other choices are rhododendron, evergreen privet, ivy, yew, American box tree, hedge euonymous, barberry and pieris. These can be planted around the perimeter of the garden for privacy, or they can be located throughout the property, with their different colors creating the effect of a tapestry that looks as beautiful under a blanket of snow as it does surrounded by flowers.

◆ Shrubbery's combination of strength and softness can be the perfect solution when setting up visual boundaries in the landscape. In this garden (*above*), clipped yews buffer a stone wall separating the upper and lower levels of the lawn. And on more than one occasion the bushes saved someone from stepping over the edge!

◆ Evergreens are always dressed, giving steadfast richness to the garden. During the coldest months of the year they patiently furnish the landscape all by themselves. Come spring, they provide a broad background for the first colorful flowers of the season. A small arboretum of Japanese cutleaf maple, cedars, pines and spruce give this deep-woods birdbath (*opposite*) year-round privacy. The stone bench nearby is a convenient perch from which to observe these daily ablutions.

A natural, or wild, garden is easy to maintain and brings an idyllic look to your property. If there is already an untamed meadow or a stretch of woodland in your landscape, you may need to do little more than add a serpentine path made of earth or paved with native stone. If you add a stone path, consider planting a variety of sedums and small bulbs between the rocks. But if you plan to cultivate a wild garden from scratch, it's important to familiarize yourself with the plants that are native to your area. These are the varieties that will naturally grow best in your soil.

Your wild garden can be as elaborate as a woodland garden complete with a delicate ground cover of violets and wintergreen as well as delicately beautiful wild flowers such as Dutchman's breeches and hepaticas. A mixture of sun-loving ferns on the perimeter of the woodland creates a soft transition from open yard to forest. The coiled heads of ferns have an architectural, sculptural look in early spring.

To bring additional visual interest to your wild or woodland garden, add rocks of varying sizes and allow native vines such as Virginia creeper to grow over them. If your property has no trees, you might consider planting a wild meadow filled with sun-loving flowers. A mixture of wild flowers in varied colors will attract industrious bumblebees. Butterflies also love wild-flower meadows and are drawn by coneflowers, gold-enrod, joe-pye weed and clover. As the seasons change in the meadow garden, so do the colors and textures of the plants. During the warm-weather months, the meadow garden is a kaleidoscope of bright colors. In autumn wild grasses and late-season flowers have a softer patina and can be harvested for autumn wreaths and delicate-toned arrangements.

◆ Poppies love the sun and can tolerate dry conditions. In France (*right*), fields of wild Flanders and California poppies, bachelors buttons and clarkia are a common sight, casting their colors in a brilliant display. One advantage of planting a garden with these exuberant flowers is that their intense colors can be seen from a distance, for instance from kitchen and bedroom windows.

◆ Symmetry is the hallmark of the small formal garden (*left, above*), where a stone birdbath with a lily pond at its feet takes center stage. The back edge of the garden proper is wreathed by a half-ring of roses. Silvery, low-growing dusty miller plants arranged in single file fill either side of the grassy central path. The bench looks so Victorian, one feels compelled to use it for only the most old-fashioned pursuits—catching up on correspondence, sewing and the like.

◆ This is an American garden (*left, below*), but the vast lawn with its ornamental fountain and broad stone steps has all the hallmarks of an English enclave. Tall pines frame the scene.

◆ Precise and orderly, the formal garden has a tranquility all its own. Witness this standard variegated English holly tree (*opposite*) holding forth from a terra-cotta square, with carefully clipped balls of golden-edged boxwood and green miniature ivy forming a frame beneath.

◆ Romance and roses are inexorably linked. Perhaps that's why this slightly overgrown, tangled web of a rose garden (*left*) is so beguiling. The owner of this Georgia garden chooses roses for their romantic quality, insisting "they must look right in a bouquet." Soft pink 'New Dawn' roses cling to the iron trellis arching over a stone footpath. The glazed, clay-colored urn collects rainwater, which is used to nourish the garden during dry spells.

◆ A rock garden will test the gardener's ingenuity, but the glorious results make all the hours of careful planning worthwhile. In the side yard (*opposite, above*) a stockade-style fence scrambles along the far property line, setting up a weathered backdrop for taller plants and those that must be staked. In the rocky soil between the fence and the stone retaining wall, all manner of plants—Japanese and Siberian iris, lady's mantle, coral bells, highbush blueberry, lamb's ears, yarrow, pinks and violets—have found a foothold. The yard terraces down from the fenceline, past the retaining wall, to a shady expanse (*opposite, below*). Despite the less-than-ideal soil here, a colorful array of ledge-loving flowers poke through the patches of embedded stones. Instead of a bone, this dog prefers to chew on yarrow (*above*).

Rock gardens are charming additions to the yard and can take many forms, ranging from the rugged, craggy alpine garden to the serene Japanese-style garden in which each plant and rock is painstakingly placed. Some homeowners are fortunate enough to have existing rock outcroppings on their property. If this is the case and the rocks are located in an area of the property that is convenient for gardening, then all you need do is clear off existing vegetation around the spot and begin planting your rock garden. Supplement existing stone with boulders and rocks of harmonious textures and colorations. A small scattering of rocks on the property can be enhanced by adding a boulder as a focal point.

If you wish to create a rock garden where no stony outcroppings or ledges exist, be sure to first study a natural rock formation to see how it is structured. Rock gardens should look as though the rocks are all connected below ground. Mass stones together to create a bold, natural-looking effect rather than scattering them about randomly on the property. If the rock garden is constructed on a sloping site, remember that in natural rock formations, more rock is exposed as the grade becomes higher. Try to use only stone that is indigenous to your area in your rockery, which will make the effect even more believable.

Greenhouses protect delicate plants in winter and allow the gardener to get an early start on spring planting by sheltering seedlings indoors. Before you start looking at catalogs and plans for greenhouses, consider whether you have a suitable place on your property for such a structure. Except in the Deep South and the Southwest, greenhouses need to be situated where they have full sun for at least half a day in the fall and winter. Filtered sun from tall, deciduous shade trees is all that is needed for spring and summer.

There are two basic greenhouse styles. The free-standing type is the traditional design and should have its longest sides facing east and west to take full advantage of light. A lean-to is attached to another structure. When placed on the south of a building, a lean-to is much less costly to heat in the winter and makes a delightful addition to a living area.

While heating may seem all-important in the greenhouse, shading and cooling are just as vital to success. From midspring until early fall, most home greenhouses require some kind of shading, which may be as simple as planting grapevines around the outside, or as complicated as whitewashing and using lath frames, roll-up bamboo curtains or plastic shading.

◆ Bell jars nurture new-born seedlings in the brightness of this peak-roofed greenhouse (*opposite*). The herringbone-patterned bricks on the floor are practical and decorative at the same time.

◆ Because the greenhouse (*above, left*) can get very warm at times, the owner planted a row of espaliered dwarf fruit trees to softly filter the light. Plants get their start in the greenhouse and then get shipped out to one of the beds outdoors. An old wheelbarrow with collapsible sides awaits its next assignment on the brick patio nearby.

◆ This little white greenhouse and attached gardener's cottage (*above, right*) share a common chimney that warms a bit of both. The buildings are old and have served several generations of this family through the years. Diamond-shaped grillwork in the windows of the cottage is repeated on the greenhouse door, visually linking the two structures. The cottage is crowned with a wreath of Boston ivy, which covers the gutters and adds a gala topping that turns scarlet in autumn. Outside in the yard, a bountiful garden grows.

◆ As the act of gardening is a great joy, the appreciation of the garden is just as pleasing. A garden truly becomes complete when it is delighted in . . . luxuriated in . . . indulged in. And for the gardener, savoring the growing of things has an enormous reward, for there is real benefit to a lingering look over the plot to fantasize and plan new developments. Placing a garden seat at a point from which flowers, shrubs and trees are seen to advantage will guarantee many hours of such soothing contemplation. (Other considerations are the sun's path and the patterns of the wind.) The seat may reflect the garden's style, or be a counterpoint to it, so long as it is comfortable. This intricate white iron bench (*above*) might have been woven by spiders. Framed to perfection by a shady nook of hydrangea, the bench is a favored location for leisurely reading.

◆ A chipped wicker chair and green garden bench (*above, left*) offer a fine, secluded vantage point for enjoying urban greenery. Another lure of this garden spot: the scent of flowering tobacco and roses that pervades the air.

◆ The years and the elements have tempered this wood bench (*above, right*), leaving it with an exquisitely weathered green-painted finish. English garden seats such as this add an elegant note to even a wild garden, with wild mint that has grown up through the slots.

◆ Gardeners wanted; no plot of land required. That's the beauty of container gardening. An old millstone set into this backyard lawn (*opposite, above*) is the platter for a variety of pots, each one filled with a plant that would rather live in close quarters than be out on its own. The climbing plant has a ready-made trellis: three pliable branches lashed together, tepee-style, at the top. The greenhouse (*opposite, below left*) is skirted by a row of terra-cotta pots enclosed in a wooden trough. A collection of watering cans stands alongside. Side by side, the plants form a leafy hedge. The individual pots can also be separated and easily transported to brighten other corners of the property when necessary. A dwarf myrtle (*opposite, below right*) competes for height with a freestanding shelf of potted alpine and succulent plants that thrive on the sunny side of a house. A majestic old wicker urn on a pedestal (*above*) sprouts dark blue-purple browallia in a backyard knoll, for instant garden-party atmosphere.

Container gardening is an ancient practice. The technique has been raised to the level of fine art in the Orient, where dwarfed bonsai trees have been passed from one generation to another. Today, limited by time and space, we are using container gardens in ways never dreamed of by the ancients. Plants and containers become accessories to complement exterior living. Not only can container plantings be changed from season to season for continuous color, they can also be arranged, moved, mixed and matched as the occasion may dictate. The scented pots of roses used to decorate a terrace room for Sunday brunch can line a front walk to welcome guests in the evening. Success depends upon choosing plants and containers that work well separately, in groupings and in a variety of locations.

Since nurseries everywhere cultivate trees, shrubs and flowers in containers, it's easy to shop for suitable plants to grow this way. While it may be difficult to envision a gangly bareroot rosebush in a decorative terra-cotta pot, it's a simple matter to buy a rose already growing in a pot or can and transplant it at home to a container of your choice. Other shrubby plants for containers in the sun include viburnum, Chinese hibiscus, lilac, dwarf crape myrtle and hydrangea. For a partially shaded place, select from camellias, azaleas, gardenias and pieris.

◆ The accoutrements of a gardener's craft have a sculptural beauty all their own. The best arrangements are the simplest and are rooted in practicality. A row of trugs and forks lines this garage wall (*opposite*). Spades and shovels get a rust-proofing bath in an old barrel full of oiled sand.

◆ Inventive gardeners find unusual places to store the tools of their craft (*this page*). The best place for long-nosed watering cans is under the old farm table. Instead of storing her collection of terra-cotta urns in a cupboard (*above, left*), this gardener places them among her plants, where they can be admired from all angles. Clay pots in all shapes and sizes (*above, right*) harbor a variety of plants. *En masse*, they make a greater statement than they would individually. An elephant and a galvanized watering can turn their backs on each other on opposite ends of a park bench (*center*), separated by a topsy-turvy collection of clay containers that aren't being used right now. In another garden (*below, left*), ornamental pots—some already filled with pansies and foxglove—await being set out in the yard. The rusty old pump still works (*below, right*), so these stone ledges are a favorite watering spot for plants. Sometimes a night's gusty winds blow over a plant or two, but no permanent damage is done.

◆ Irises form a frilly fence
at the end of this Connecticut garden (*left*), where the
owner wanted to delineate
the transition between the
yard and open woods. Irises
are early bloomers and as
sure a sign of spring as
robins on the lawn.

◆ A duet of delicate white
German irises arch splen-
didly against a flattering
background of 'Crater Lake'
veronicas (*above*).

◆ A riot of color give this garden (*left*) its exuberance. But beneath its carefree appearance there lies a careful plan. In the fashion of Gertrude Jekyll, a famous turn-of-the-century English gardener and writer, plants are grown in individual groups. Each group can be savored on it own; viewed as a whole, a charming landscape is created. The weathered old barn in the background is a handy potting shed.

◆ A rose garden offers unlimited opportunities to create a colorful landscape, but the palette is unique. Because roses are so fragile, their soft shades seem especially subtle, and their brilliant tones rich as jewels. And depending on the colors they're next to, the effect is amplified. These roses (*opposite, above*) prove the point. Two oval beds of roses grace a back lawn with their contrasting colors. In the front bed, the owners grouped all the roses in delicate shades. In the second bed, white peonies are a foil for dark pink roses, the contrast setting off the beauty of each. Close-ups of a blushing peony (*opposite, below, left*) and deep pink roses (*opposite, below, right*) magnify their delicate complexions.

RESOURCE DIRECTORY

The following list comprises sources of items for the yard, including plant and seed suppliers. There are also listings for companies that make outdoor furniture and garden structures as well as ornaments and containers for the yard. Selecting from this full range of products, the gardener should be well equipped to plan every aspect of the outdoor room.

Every company included sells through the mail and, except for the antiques stores, all will send a catalog on request. Since the stock in antiques stores changes frequently, you should call or write describing the item you want.

GENERAL CATALOGS

Abercrombie & Fitch
Mailing List Preference Service
P.O. Box 70858
Houston, TX 77270

Pool floats, deck chairs, wicker picnic baskets and such backyard games as croquet, horseshoes, miniature golf and volleyball.

Brookstone Company
127 Vose Farm Road
Peterborough, NH 03458

General stock includes garden tools, sundials, furniture, flags, swings and Pawley's Island hammocks.

Clapper's
1125 Washington Street
West Newton, MA 02165

Classic American and English wood furniture, a wide variety of well-made hand tools, waterproof planters and outdoor lighting sets.

David Kay Gifts for Home and Garden
4509 Taylor Lane
Cleveland, OH 44128

Gifts and gadgets for the backyard, including stone garden pets, birdhouses and seeds for clover, grasses and flowers.

Gardener's Eden
P.O. Box 7307
San Francisco, CA 94120

Rustic furniture, trellises and arbors, planters and a good variety of garden ornaments.

Gardener's Supply Company
128 Intervale Road
Burlington, VT 05401

A serious gardener's catalog, offering such items as plastic cold frames, composters, tillers and irrigation systems.

Hammacher Schlemmer
147 East 57th Street
New York, NY 10022

The unusual and hard to find: folding portable grills, solar-powered outdoor lights, motorized wheelbarrows, infrared security lights, pool games and outdoor speakers.

Hen-Feathers and Company
10 Balligomingo Road
Gulph Mills, PA 19428

Birdbaths, sundials, planters, pots, troughs, figures in lead, terra-cotta or verdigris, benches and garden tools.

The Kinsman Company
River Road
Point Pleasant, PA 18950

Tools and accessories for the gardener, including plant supports, cold frames, compost bins, arbors and arches.

The Nature Company
P.O. Box 2310
Berkeley, CA 94702

General selection of stone birdbaths, Soleri bells, sundials, bird feeders and pool toys.

The Plow and Hearth
560 Main Street
Madison, VA 22727

Green River garden tools, various birdhouses, birdbaths and birdfeeders as well as outdoor furniture covers.

Renovator's Supply
Millers Falls, MA 01349

Reproductions of Victorian hardware and accessories, including spigots, sundials, lights, birdhouses and weather vanes.

Smith and Hawken
25 Corte Madera
Mill Valley, CA 94941

English and Japanese garden tools, irrigation and sprinkler systems, classic wood furniture and planters of fiberglass and plastic.

Walpole Woodworkers
767 East Street
Walpole, MA 02081

Rustic cedar furniture, including swings and picnic sets, cabanas and other small buildings, and a wide range of accessories from weather vanes to mailboxes.

Winterthur Catalogue
Winterthur Museum and Gardens
Winterthur, DE 19735

A general gift catalog that offers a variety of planters and some rare shrubs and trees from the Winterthur gardens.

Wolfman-Gold & Good Company
484 Broome Street
New York, NY 10013

Planters, latticework window boxes, statuary, elaborate birdhouses, gardening tools, picnic baskets, garden furniture and umbrellas.

ANTIQUES

Irreplaceable Artifacts
14 Second Avenue
New York, NY 10003

Antique stone benches, friezes and statuary, usually one-of-a-kind.

Lost City Arts
275 Lafayette Street
New York, NY 10012

Extensive collection of antique accessories for the garden: urns, columns, furniture, cast-iron fences, lamps, friezes and weather vanes.

Urban Archaeology
285 Lafayette Street
New York, NY 10012

Antique statuary, furniture, ornaments in stone, iron, and terra-cotta, wrought-iron fences and gates.

ORNAMENTS & ARCHITECTURAL DETAILS

Ballard Designs
2148-J Hills Avenue
Atlanta, GA 30318

Pedestals, columns, sconces and gargoyles.

Bow House, Inc.
P.O. Box 228FG1
Bolton, MA 01740

Pool and garden structures, including bridges.

Cape Cod Cupola
78 State Road, Route 6
North Dartmouth, MA 02747

Hundreds of traditional, handmade aluminum and copper weather vanes, as well as cupolas, wall eagles, mailbox signs, weather stations and bird feeders.

Cassidy Brothers Forge, Inc.
U.S. Route 1
Rowley, MA 01969

Custom architectural ironwork.

Cumberland Woodcraft Company, Inc.
P.O. Drawer 609
Carlisle, PA 17013

Standard and custom corbels, capitals, gables and architectural trim, as well as gazebos in Victorian patterns.

The English Garden, Inc.
652 Glenbrook Road
Stamford, CT 06906

Planters, trellises, gazebos, birdhouses, seats and pavilions.

Florentine Craftsmen
46–24 28th Street
Long Island City, NY 11101

Ornamental metalwork, including fountains, staues, birdbaths, astrolabes, sundials and urns.

The Gazebo and Porchworks
728 Ninth Avenue SW
Puyallup, WA 98371

Victorian gazebos, decorative screen doors, porch swing, gingerbread and turned columns.

Haas Wood and Ivory Works, Inc.
64 Clementina Street
San Francisco, CA 94105

Custom and stock wood trim, brackets and columns; will work from client's drawings.

Haddonstone of England
Represented by Exotic Blossoms
P.O. Box 2436
Philadelphia, PA 19147

Country garden ornaments and architectural details.

Hermitage Garden Pools
P.O. Box 361
Canastoga, NY 13032

Fiberglass rocks, pools, waterfalls, wooden bridges and waterwheels.

Huston and Company
P.O. Box 380 G
Poland Spring, ME 04274

Custom landscape structures.

Kenneth Lynch & Sons
P.O. Box 488
Wilton, CT 06897

Extensive range of fountains and pools, statuary, gates, planters, benches, finials and sundials.

Moultrie Manufacturing Company
P.O. Drawer 1179
Moultrie, GA 31776

Cast-aluminum columns with various capitals and bases, both standard and custom.

Nampara Gardens
2004 Golf Course Road
Bayside, CA 95524

General selection of garden ornaments.

Robert Compton Ltd.
Star Route, Box 6
Bristol, VT 05443

Stoneware fountains.

Robinson Iron
P.O. Box 1119
Alexander City, AL 35010

Cast-iron fountains and furniture.

Southern Statuary & Stone
3401 Fifth Avenue South
Birmingham, AL 35222

Statues and planters.

Sun Designs
P.O. Box 206
Delafield, WI 53018

Gazebo kits.

The Sundial Company
P.O. Box 824
Cathedral Station
New York, NY 10023-0824

Sundials.

Sundials and More
1901 North Narragansett Avenue
Chicago, IL 60639

Garden ornaments.

Weatherking Products, Inc.
1485 South County Trail
East Greenwich, RI 02818

In-ground and portable pools, spas and
hot tubs.

Western Wood Products Association
Department PS23M
1500 Yeon Building
Portland, OR 97204

Deck design kit covers basic and design
options, including planning grid.

Wind and Weather
P.O. Box 2320
Mendocino, CA 95460

Sundials, weather vanes, weather
instruments.

Windleaves Weathervanes
7560 Morningside Drive
Indianapolis, IN 46240

Selection of weather vanes.

Worthington Group, Ltd.
P.O. Box 53101
Atlanta, GA 30355

Pine pedestals in a variety of finishes, and
columns and capitals in assorted sizes and
styles.

Vintage Woodworks
Box 1157
513 South Adams
Fredericksburg, TX 78624

Victorian and country gingerbread trim
from pine and a Victorian-style gazebo.

BARBECUES & GRILLS

Barbecues Galore
14048 East Firestone Boulevard
Santa Fe Springs, CA 90670

Extensive selection of smokers and gas,
charcoal, electric and infrared barbecues,
as well as accessories.

Brookstone Company
127 Vose Farm Road
Peterborough, NH 03458

Barbecues and barbecue cooking
equipment.

Chef's Catalogue
3215 Commercial Avenue
Northbrook, IL 60062

Selection of barbecues and grills, equipment and mesquite chips.

Cook'n Cajun
P.O. Box 3726
Shreveport, LA 71133

Water smokers and grills.

Grillworks, Inc.
1211 Ferdon Road
Ann Arbor, MI 48104

Movable, wood-fueled rotisserie/grill.

BIRDHOUSES & FEEDERS

Duncraft
33 Fisherville Road
Penacook, NH 03303

Specialist bird feeder, birdbath, birdhouse
and bird feed supply source, with houses
designed exclusively for purple martins.

Hyde Bird Feeder Company
P.O. Box 168
Waltham, MA 02254

Hummingbird bird feeders, hanging and
post feeders and window feeders.

The Plow and Hearth
560 Main Street
Madison, VA 22727

Various birdbaths, bird feeders and birdhouses in concrete, aluminum and wood,
including a house that can be raised and
lowered on a pole.

Wild Bird Supplies
4815 Oak Street
Crystal Lake, IL 60012

Almost everything for the bird lover:
birdhouses, bird feeders, feed, books and
records.

CHILDREN'S PLAY EQUIPMENT

Childlife Play Specialties, Inc.
P.O. Box 527
Holliston, MA 01746

Modular wood jungle gyms, swings, slides,
treehouses, playhouses and sandboxes.

Hearth Song
P.O. Box B
Sebastopol, CA 95472

Various old-fashioned children's toys and
games, including gym set, playhouse,
wind chimes and picnic hamper.

Walpole Woodworkers
767 East Street
Walpole, MA 02081

Jungle gyms, sandboxes, and furniture made of cedar, as well as freestanding wood playhouses.

Woodplay
P.O. Box 27904
Raleigh, NC 27611

Modular redwood jungle gyms, seesaws, treehouses with swings, swing and slide sets.

FURNITURE & PLANTERS

Amish Outlet
R.D. 1, Box 102
New Wilmington, PA 16142

Bent hickory and plain oak tables, single and double rockers and gliders.

Barlow Tyrie, Inc.
65 Great Valley Parkway
Malvern, PA 19355

English teakwood furniture.

BenchCraft
36 New Port Drive
Wayne, PA 19087

Cast-aluminum tables and chairs, some in ornate Victorian designs; English teak chairs, tables and lounges, including white Lutyens benches.

Cape Cod Comfys
P.O. Box 15103
Seattle, WA 98115

West Coast source of unfinished Adirondack chairs in pine or cedar, as well as porch swings.

Charleston Battery Bench, Inc.
191 King Street
Charleston, SC 29401

Cast-iron and cypress benches.

Chippendale Home and Garden Furnishings
3401 Fifth Avenue South
Birmingham, AL 35222

Easily assembled cypress outdoor furniture.

Country Casual
17317 Germantown Road
Germantown, MD 20874

Mostly English tables, chairs, benches, swings and planters in teak, including classic benches.

Country Loft
South Shore Park
Hingham, MA 02043

Rope hammocks.

The Greenery
3237 Pierce Street
San Francisco, CA 94123

Artisan-carved redwood furniture washed with cement to look sun-bleached, including benches, chairs, lounges and tables.

Hangouts
1-800-HANGOUT for brochure
1-800-442-2533 for order

Mayan and Brazilian hand-woven hammocks of cotton and nylon.

Irving & Jones
Village Center
Colebrook, CT 06021

Reproductions of traditional garden furniture, twig furniture and nineteenth-century English furniture in wrought iron.

La Lune Collection
241 North Broadway
Milwaukee, WI 53202

Bent-willow chaises, tables and sofas with canvas cushions.

Lazy Hill Farm Designs
P.O. Box 235
Colerain, NC 27924

Handcrafted garden accessories, including birdhouses.

Kingsley–Bate
P.O. Box 6797
Arlington, VA 22206

Hand-carved teak furniture.

Lister Teak, Inc.
561 Exton Commons
Exton, PA 19341

Traditional English teak tables, chairs, benches and planters, all imported.

Daniel Mack Rustic Furnishings
3280 Broadway
New York, NY 10025

Imaginative twig furniture, each piece made to order and one-of-a-kind.

Moultrie Manufacturing Co.
P.O. Drawer 1179
Moultrie, GA 31768

Cast-aluminum reproductions of Victorian and Old South chairs, tables, settees and planters; special finishing is available.

Park Place
2251 Wisconsin Avenue NW
Washington, DC 20007

Victorian enameled cast-aluminum, mahogany and teak benches.

The Rocker Shop
P.O. Box 12
Marietta, GA 30061

Traditional hand-caned wood rocking chairs and footstools, porch swings and side tables.

Santa Barbara Designs
205 West Carillo Street
Santa Barbara, CA 93101

Collapsible furniture and umbrellas.

Settona Willow Company
41655 Magnolia
Murietta, CA 92362

Traditional bent-willow furniture gates and fences made to order.

Shaker Workshops
P.O. Box 1028
Concord, MA 01742

Shaker-style rockers and chairs in kits or already assembled.

Unique Simplicities
P.O. Box 1185
New Paltz, NY 12561

Reasonably priced Adirondack furniture; hammock chairs and hammocks.

United Outdoor Products
120 South Raymond Avenue
Pasedena, CA 91105

Classic teak furniture and market umbrellas.

Van Klassens
4619B Central Avenue Road
Knoxville, TN 37912

Fine garden furniture; mahogany protected with marine paint (settees, benches, chairs, tables, rockers, swings).

Wave Hill Lawn Furniture
675 West 252nd Street
Bronx, NY 10471

Unfinished pine lawn chair based on modernistic Gerrit Rietveld design.

Willow Works
209 Glen Cove Avenue
Sea Cliff, NY 11579

Bent-willow chairs, lounges, swings and plant stands, stripped, dyed or plain.

Wood Classics, Inc.
R.D. #1, Box 455E
High Falls, NY 12440

Mahogany and teak benches, chairs, picnic tables, and lounges; swings, poolside rockers and Adirondack furniture.

Zona
97 Greene Street
New York, NY 10012

English teak furniture, plus accessories and furnishings from the American Southwest.

GREENHOUSES, GAZEBOS, GARDEN BUILDINGS & DECKS

Amdega Conservatories
Amdega LTD
Dept US03/9
Boston Design Center
Boston, MA 02210

Victorian-style conservatories in western red cedar with insulating or antisolar glass.

G.S. Andrea, Inc.
11–40 45th Road
Long Island City, NY 11101

Fiberglass, fully screened cabins.

Cedar Gazebos, Inc.
10432 Lyndale
Melrose Park, IL 60164

Selection of gazebos.

Columbine
P.O. Box 212, Route 3
Blairstown, NJ 07825

Modular terra-cotta columns that assemble to make pergolas and gazebos.

Crawford Products, Inc.
301 Winter Street
West Hanover, MA 02239

Build-a-deck hardware kit.

Dalton Pavillions
7260 Oakley Street
Philadelphia, PA 19111

Pavilions and gazebos.

Four Seasons Greenhouses
425 Smith Street
Farmingdale, NY 11735

Aluminum-framed sunrooms and greenhouses with single-, double- or triple-glazing.

HomeScapes
22121 Crystal Creek Boulevard SE
Bothell, WA 98021

Prefabricated gazebos.

Janco Greenhouses and Glass Structures
JA Nearing Co.
9390 Davis Avenue
Laurel, MD 20707

Greenhouses, solariums and sun rooms with aluminum framing.

Lord & Burnham
2 Main Street
Irvington, NY 10533

Extensive range of aluminum-framed sun rooms and greenhouses.

Machin Designs, Inc.
557 Danbury Road (Route 7)
Wilton, CT 06877

Architectural details and conservatories.

Texas Greenhouse Co.
2524 White Settlement Road
Fort Worth, TX 76107

A greenhouse manufacturer.

Vintage Gazebos
P.O. Box 1157
Fredricksburg, TX 75474

Reproductions of antique gazebos.

Vixen Hill Gazebos
Elverson, PA 19520

Pre-engineered gazebos for easily assembly.

Walpole Woodworkers
767 East Street
Walpole, MA 02081

Several small wood garden sheds and buildings in kit form; also cabanas, boathouses and stables.

Zytco Solariums
825 Denison Street, Unit 16
Markham, Ontario L3R 5E4
Canada

Greenhouses.

LIGHTING

Doner Design, Inc.
2175 Beaver Valley Pike
New Providence, RI 17560

Handcrafted copper landscape lights.

Hanover Lantern
470 High Street
Hanover, PA 17331

Landscape lighting.

Genie House

P.O. Box 2478
Red Lion Road
Vincentown, NJ 08088

Handcrafted garden lamps in solid brass and copper.

Hammerworks

6 Fremont Street
Worcester, MA 01603

Post- and wall-mounted electric lanterns, handmade and finished in copper or brass.

Philip Hawk & Company

159 East College Avenue
Pleasant Gap, PA 16823

Stone lanterns hand-carved in granite.

Heritage Lanterns

70A Main Street
Yarmouth, ME 04096

Pewter, cooper and brass lanterns in Colonial styles; post- and wall-mounted models.

Idaho Wood

P.O. Box 488
Sandpoint, ID 83864

Cedar landscape and wall lights.

Popovitch and Associates Incorporated

346 Ashland Avenue
Pittsburgh, PA 15228

Unusual outdoor lamps with copper stems and ceramic globes come bell-shaped, mushroom-shaped and bud-shaped.

Rab Electrical Manufacturing Company, Inc.

321 Ryder Avenue
Bronx, NY 10451

Security and general outdoor lighting.

The Washington Copper Works

South Street
Washington, CT 06793

Handcrafted copper lanterns.

Wendelighting

2445 North Naomi Street
Burbank, CA 91504

Plant lights, tree illumination and other kinds of landscape lighting.

FLOWERS, SHRUBS & TREES

Ahrens Nursery and Plant Lab

R.R. 1, Box FN 89
Huntingberg, IN 47542

Offers berries, fruits, herbs and tools.

The Antique Rose Emporium

Box 143, Route 5
Brenham, TX 77833

Good selection of old-fashioned roses.

Beaverlodge Nurseries

Box 127
Beaverlodge, Alberta TOH OCO
Canada

Large selection of hardy ornamental and fruit trees, shrubs and perennials.

Kurt Bluemel Inc.

2740 Greene Lane
Baldwin, MD 21013

Over one hundred varieties of ornamental grasses and rushes, as well as bamboos, ferns and perennials.

Bluestone Perennials, Inc.

7211 Middle Road
Madison, OH 44057

Small, inexpensive plants, with a wide selection of shrubs and perennials.

Burpee Seed Co.

Warminster, PA 18991

Wide range of vegetable and flower seeds, as well as shrubs and fruit trees.

Carlson's Gardens

P.O. Box 305
South Salem, NY 10590

Selection of azaleas, mountain laurels and rhododendrons.

Crownsville Nursery

1241 Generals Highway
Crownsville, MD 21032

Large selection of well-grown perennials.

Eco-Gardens

P.O. Box 1227
Decatur, GA 30031

Herbaceous plants grown from seeds collected in the mountains.

Herb Gathering, Inc.

5742 Kenwood Avenue
Kansas City, MO 64110

Herb plants and seeds and hard-to-find vegetables.

Holbrook Farm & Nursery

Route 2, Box 223 B
Fletcher, NC 28732

Medium-size plants.

Jackson and Perkins Co.
83-A Rose Lane
Medford, OR 97501

Roses and fruit trees.

Klehm Nursery
P.O. Box 197, Route 5
South Barrington, IL 60010

Extensive selection of bearded iris, day lilies, hostas and peonies.

Lamb Nurseries
East 101 Sharpe Avenue
Spokane, WA 99202

Many unusual perennials.

Lilypons Water Gardens
P.O. Box 10
Lilypons, MD 21717

Water lilies, water grasses and bog plants, ornamental fish, ponds and pond supplies.

Logee's Greenhouses
55 North Street
Danielson, CT 06239

Geraniums and begonias; herbs, mosses and ferns; perennials.

Mileager's Gardens
4838 Douglas
Racine, WI 53402

Unusual perennials and a large selection of roses; one of the few nurseries to sell plants rather than seeds of native prairie grasses.

Nor'East Miniature Roses, Inc.
58 Hammond Street
Rawley, MA 01969

Wide selection of miniature roses.

Oliver Nurseries, Inc.
1159 Bronson Road
Fairfield, CT 06430

Selection of rock garden plants, conifers, wall gardens, general landscaping and reeds.

Pickering Nurseries
670 Kingston Road
Pickering, Ontario L1V 1A6
Canada

Good selection of old-fashioned roses.

Roses of Yesterday and Today
802 Brown's Valley Road
Watsonville, CA 95076

Extensive range of antique roses.

John Scheepers, Inc.
63 Wall Street
New York, NY 10005

Seasonal selections of daffodils, tulips and other bulbs.

Solar Green Ltd.
R.R. 1, Box 115 A
Moore, ID 83255

Alpine and rock garden plants.

Swan Island Dahlias
P.O. Box 800
Candy, OR 97013

Dwarf and giant dahlias.

Transplant Nursery

Parkertown Road
Livonia, GA 30053

Specializes in hardy wild azaleas grown from seed; also have cutting plants from selected varieties.

Twombley Nursery, Inc.

163 Barn Hill Road
Monroe, CT 06468

Selection of over 50,000 dwarf and rare conifers, rock garden plants and perennials.

Van Bourgondien Bros.

P.O. Box A
Babylon, NY 11702

Good selection of Dutch bulbs.

Van Ness Water Gardens

2460 North Euclid Avenue
Upland, CA 91768

Water lilies, fountains, filters and pond supplies.

Vermont Wildflower Farm

P.O. Box 5
Charlotte, VT 05445

Wild flower species and mixes.

Vick's Wildgardens

Conshohocken State Road
P.O. Box 115
Gladwyne, PA 19035

One of America's oldest family-run nurseries; specializes in wild flowers and ferns.

Waterford Gardens

74 East Allerdale Road
Saddle River, NJ 07458

A water garden source for pools, accessories, lilies, bog plants and ornamental fish.

Wayside Gardens

Hodges, SC 29695-0001

All-around selection of plants, bulbs, shrubs and trees; some garden tools and furniture.

We-Do Nurseries

Route 5, Box 724
Marion, NC 28752

Nursery-grown native wild flowers and unusual plants from Japan.

Weston Nurseries

Route 135, P.O. Box 186
Hopkinton, MA 01748

New England's largest listing of landscape-size trees, shrubs, perennials, flowers and fruit.

Woodland Nurseries

2152 Camilla Road
Mississauga, Ontario L5A 2K1
Canada

Alpine perennials, evergreens and especially ornamental trees; dogwoods, azaleas, rhododendrons and magnolias.

GARDENING SUPPLIES & SEEDS

Clapper Company
1121 Washington St.
Newton, MA 02165

Garden supplies.

Denman and Company
2913 Saturn St.
Suite H
Brea, CA 92621

Selection of garden tools and clothing.

Gro-Tek
South Berwick, ME 02908

Well-priced supplies for greenhouse owners.

Harris Seeds
Morton Farm
3670 Buffalo Road
Rochester, NY 14624

Vegetable and flower seeds.

Johnny's Selected Seeds
Foss Hill Road
Albion, ME 04910

Seeds for northern climates; have extensive trial gardens to test seeds; carry "heirloom varieties" of seeds passed through families for generations.

Langenbach
P.O. Box 453
Dept. 10
Blairstown, NJ 07825

Selection of finely crafted garden tools.

John D. Lyon
143 Alewife Brook Parkway
Cambridge, MA 02140

Specializes in lawn seed and garden products; connoisseur's list of special bulbs for fall planting.

Malvern Nursery
Route 2, Box 265 B
Ashville, NC 28805

Perhaps the best seed list for ornamental plants in the country.

Mellinger's
2310 West South Range Road
North Lima, OH 4452

Vast selection of gardening supplies.

Pinetree Garden Seeds
New Gloucester, ME 04260

Specializes in compact varieties, including many heirloom vegetable seeds. Special notice: rare Jenny Lind muskmelon.

Richters
Box 26
Goodwood, Ontario L0C 1A0
Canada

Exceptional source for herb seeds and plants, including many hard-to-find varieties.

Seeds Blum
Idaho City Stage
Boise, ID 83707

Large selection of heirloom seeds.

Sheperd's Garden Seeds
7389 West Zayante Road
Felton, CA 95018

Specializes in European vegetable seeds.

Slocum Water Gardens

1101 Cypress Gardens Road
Winter Haven, FL 33880

Water gardens and supplies.

Southern Exposure Seed Exchange

P.O. Box 158
North Garden, VA 22959

Seeds adaptable to solar greenhouses; also specializes in "multiplier onions" which divide underground.

Thompson & Morgan

P.O. Box 1308
Jackson, NJ 08527

Offer seeds for all common and rare flowering plants that can be grown from seed, perennials, annuals, vegetables and trees.

Vermont Bean Seed Co.

Garden Lane
Fair Haven, VT 05743

Specializes in bean and connoisseur vegetable seeds.

SPRINKLERS & IRRIGATION SYSTEMS

Gardena Inc.

6031 Culligan Way
Minnetonka, MN 55345

Sprinklers, start-up drip kits, valves, nozzles.

GardenAmerica Corp.

1815 South Roop Street
P.O. Box A
Carson City, NV 89702

Features Drip Mist watering system.

The Gilmour Group

332 West Broadway
Suite 815
Louisville, KY 40202

Sprinklers and nozzles.

Melnor Industries Inc.

Moonachie, NJ 07074

Sprinklers, timed oscillators.

L.R. Nelson Corp.

7719 North Pioneer Lane
Peoria, IL 61615

Sprinklers, timers and nozzles.

RainMatic Corporation

P.O. Box 3321
Omaha, NE 68103

Sprinklers and timers.

O.M. Scott & Sons Co.

Marysville, OH 43041

Spray wands, sprinklers.

True Temper

P.O. Box 3500
465 Railroad Avenue
Shiremanstown, PA 17011

Handheld nozzles, sprinklers, connecters, adapters, start-up sets.

PHOTOGRAPHY CREDITS

page 1: Lilo Raymond

page 2: Mick Hales

pages 4–5: Michael Dunne

page 6: (*top, left*) Christopher Irion; (*top, right, and bottom, right*) William P. Steele; (*middle, left*) John Vaughan; (*middle, right*) Langdon Clay; (*bottom, left*) Edgar de Evia

pages 8–9: Peter Margonelli

CHAPTER ONE: OUTDOOR ROOMS

pages 12–13: Michael Skott

pages 14–15: Lilo Raymond

pages 16–17: Elyse Lewin

pages 18–19: Edgar de Evia

page 20: Christopher Irion

page 21: Michael Skott

page 22: William P. Steele

page 23: Joe Standart

pages 24–25: Michael Dunne

pages 26–27: William P. Steele

pages 28–31: Michael Dunne

pages 32–33: Peter Margonelli

pages 34–35: Langdon Clay

pages 36–37: Michael Dunne

page 38: (*top*) Jerry Simpson; (*bottom*) William C. Minarich

page 39: Langdon Clay

CHAPTER TWO: ENTRANCES

pages 40–41: Peter Margonelli

page 42: Michael Skott

page 43: William B. Seitz

page 44: William P. Steele

page 45: (*top*) Lilo Raymond; (*bottom*) William P. Steele

page 46: (*top*) William P. Steele; (*bottom*) Chris Callas

page 47: Ken Druse

pages 48–49: Michael Skott

page 50: Elyse Lewin

pages 51–52: William P. Steele

page 53: James Merrell

pages 54–55: Ken Druse

pages 56–58: James Merrell

page 59: (*left*) William C. Minarich: (*right*) William P. Steele

page 60: Langdon Clay

page 61: (*left*) Lilo Raymond; (*right*) Jeff McNamara

pages 62–63: Judith Watts Wilson

pages 64–67: Michael Dunne

CHAPTER THREE: PORCHES & PATIOS

pages 68–69: Lilo Raymond

page 70: Judith Watts Wilson

page 71: Lilo Raymond

pages 72–73: William B. Seitz

pages 74–75: Michael Dunne

page 76: Tom Yee

page 77: Michael Dunne

page 78: Lilo Raymond

page 79: Joshua Greene

pages 80–82: Lilo Raymond

page 83: Peter Margonelli

page 84: Tom Yee

page 85: Joshua Greene

pages 86–87: Michael Skott

pages 88–89: Tom Yee

pages 90–91: Langdon Clay

pages 92–93: John Vaughan

pages 94–95: Mick Hales

page 95: Feliciano

pages 96–99: James Merrell

pages 100–101: Michael Dunne

pages 102–103: Kari Haavisto

pages 104–105: Michael Skott

pages 106–107: Kari Haavisto

pages 108–109: Elyse Lewin

page 110: Tom Yee

page 111: Elyse Lewin

pages 112–113: Lilo Raymond

CHAPTER FOUR:
SWIMMING POOLS

pages 114–115: Michael Dunne
page 116: William C. Minarich
page 117: Michael Skott
pages 118–121: Langdon Clay
pages 122–123: Elyse Lewin
page 125: Jon Elliot
pages 126–127: Joshua Greene
pages 128–129: Michael Dunne
pages 130–131: Kari Haavisto
pages 132–133: Joe Standart
pages 134–135: Michael Skott
pages 136–137: Elyse Lewin

CHAPTER FIVE:
LITTLE RETREATS

pages 138–139: Mick Hales
page 140: Lilo Raymond
pages 141–143: Peter Margonelli
page 144: Kari Haavisto
page 145: Michael Skott
pages 146–147: Edgar de Evia
page 148: William P. Steele
page 149: (*top*) Tom Yee; (*bottom*)
    Judith Watts Wilson
pages 150–151: Elyse Lewin
pages 152–155: Judith Watts Wilson
pages 156–157: Tom Yee
pages 158–159: George Ross
pages 160–161: Tom Yee
pages 162–163: Michael Skott
page 164: Mick Hales
page 165: (*top and bottom, right*)
    Lilo Raymond; (*bottom, left*)
    Michael Skott

CHAPTER SIX:
GARDENS

pages 166–167: Mick Hales
page 168: Tom Yee
pages 169–171: William B. Seitz
page 172: (*top*) Judith Watts Wilson;
    (*bottom*) William P. Steele
page 173: (*top*) Michael Skott;
    (*bottom*) Lilo Raymond
page 174: Lilo Raymond
page 175: Kari Haavisto
page 176: Lilo Raymond
pages 176–177: Mick Hales
pages 178–179: Edgar de Evia
pages 180–181: Lilo Raymond
page 182: Michael Dunne
page 183: Chris Callas
pages 184–185: James Merrell
page 186: Michael Dunne
page 187: Edgar de Evia
page 188: Peter Margonelli
page 189: Michael Skott
pages 190–191: Michael Dunne
page 192: Lilo Raymond
pages 193–195: Mick Hales
pages 196–197: Peter Margonelli
page 198: Edgar de Evia
page 199: (*left*) Edgar de Evia; (*right*)
    Lilo Raymond
page 200: Kari Haavisto
page 201: James Merrell

page 202: (*top and bottom, right*)
    Peter Margonelli; (*bottom, left*)
    Edgar de Evia
page 203: Tom Yee
page 204: Edgar de Evia
page 205: (*top and bottom, right*)
    Edgar de Evia; (*middle*) William
    B. Seitz; (*bottom, left*) Tom Yee
pages 206–207: William P. Steele
page 208: Lilo Raymond
page 209: William P. Steele

page 210: Elyse Lewin
pages 211–212: Lilo Raymond
page 214: Michael Skott
page 215: John Vaughan
page 216: Judith Watts Wilson
page 217: Lilo Raymond
pages 218–219: William P. Steele
pages 220–221: Tom Yee

ACKNOWLEDGEMENTS

The kind and generous contributions of a great many people, uncredited on these pages, were tapped to produce the gardens and outdoor settings featured here. Surely no book of this nature could have been assembled without the participation of each of these talented individuals.

Among the designers and homeowners represented are: Thomas Bartlett, Audrey and Richard Bisgood, Hugo Bosc, Nancy Braithwaite, Dan Carithers, Sybil Connolly, John Cottrell, Frankie and Tench Coxe, Patti and Ciro Cozzi, Heather Croner, Abby Darer, Princess Marie-Sol de la Tour d'Auvergne, Maria G. Ehrlich, Stephen Farish, Isabel and Winston Fowlkes, Barbara Gallup, Bill Goldsmith, Randall Harwood, Mary and Mark Inabnit, Jennifer and George Lang, Ira Howard Levy, Joy and Robert K. Lewis, Wendy and Daniel O'Brien, Josef Pricci, John Rogers, Richard Ryan, Harriet and Sev Sorensen, Tommy Simpson and Missy Stevens, Sophie and Jean-Marie Thibault, Cornelia Wickens, Ron Wilson.

The work of four gifted architects is shown in this book without reference to their invaluable design input: Deborah Berke, Walter Chatham, Robert Orr and Melanie Taylor.

A number of important *House Beautiful* contributors were instrumental in shaping the success of key projects as published in the magazine: Marybeth Weston Bergman, Ken Druse, Norma Skurka Kimmel, Nancy Goslee Power.

Last but by no means least, the creative input of present and former *House Beautiful* editorial staff members deserves recognition, for this book is a true reflection of the energy, vision and extraordinary attention to detail they brought to each project: Sarah Belk, Al Braverman, Dara Caponigro, Katrin Tolleson Cargill, Patricia Corbin, Carolyn Englefield, Kirsten Harwood, Jason Kontos, Meredith Lubben, Kathleen Mahoney, Beverly McGuire, Rhoda Jaffin Murphy, Jody Thompson-Kennedy, Ann Wiser, Susan Zevon.